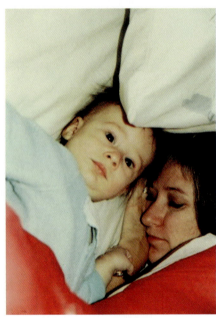

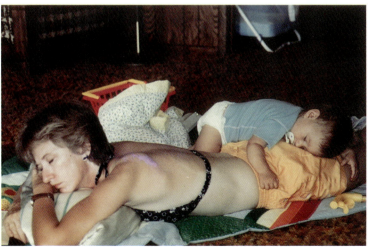

THE ESSENTIAL C.D. WRIGHT

ALSO BY C.D. WRIGHT

Casting Deep Shade: An Amble Inscribed to Beech Trees & Co.
    with photographs by Denny Moers

ShallCross

The Poet, the Lion, Talking Pictures, El Farolito, a Wedding in St. Roch, the Big Box Store, the Warp in the Mirror, Spring, Midnights, Fire & All

One With Others [a little book of her days]

Rising, Falling, Hovering

One Big Self: An Investigation

Like Something Flying Backwards: New and Selected Poems (UK)

Cooling Time: An American Poetry Vigil

One Big Self: Prisoners of Louisiana
    with photographs by Deborah Luster; text by C.D. Wright

Steal Away: Selected and New Poems

Deepstep Come Shining

Tremble

The Lost Roads Project: A Walk-in Book of Arkansas
    with photographs by Deborah Luster

Just Whistle: a valentine
    with photographs by Deborah Luster

String Light

Further Adventures with You

Translations of the Gospel Back into Tongues

Terrorism

Room Rented by a Single Woman

Alla Breve Loving

THE ESSENTIAL C.D. WRIGHT

EDITED BY FORREST GANDER AND MICHAEL WIEGERS

COPPER CANYON PRESS
PORT TOWNSEND, WASHINGTON

Copyright 2025 by the C.D. Wright Estate
Editor's Note copyright 2025 by Michael Wiegers
Introduction copyright 2025 by Forrest Gander
All rights reserved
Printed in the United States of America

Cover art: Denny Moers, *Brush on Prairie Field I, Print B,* 1996.

Copper Canyon Press is in residence at Fort Worden State Park in Port Townsend,
Washington, under the auspices of Centrum. Centrum is a gathering place for artists
and creative thinkers from around the world, students of all ages and backgrounds, and
audiences seeking extraordinary cultural enrichment.

LIBRARY OF CONGRESS CATALOGING-IN-PUBLICATION DATA
Library of Congress Cataloging-in-Publication Data
Names: Wright, C. D., 1949–2016, author. | Gander, Forrest, 1956– editor. |
Wiegers, Michael, editor.
Title: The essential C.D. Wright / edited by Forrest Gander and
Michael Wiegers.
Description: Port Townsend, Washington : Copper Canyon Press, [2025] |
Includes index. | Summary: "A collection of poems and translations drawn
from C.D. Wright's archives and from her previous books"— Provided by publisher.
Identifiers: LCCN 2024052761 (print) | LCCN 2024052762 (ebook) |
ISBN 9781556597190 (paperback) | ISBN 9781619323155 (epub)
Subjects: LCSH: American poetry—Women authors.
Classification: LCC PS3573.R497 A6 2025 (print) | LCC PS3573.R497 (ebook) |
DDC 811/.54—dc23/eng/20250203
LC record available at https://lccn.loc.gov/2024052761
LC ebook record available at https://lccn.loc.gov/2024052762

9 8 7 6 5 4 3 2 FIRST PRINTING

COPPER CANYON PRESS
Post Office Box 271
Port Townsend, Washington 98368
www.coppercanyonpress.org

FOR BRECHT

CONTENTS

xiii   Editor's Note

xvii   A Tiny Introduction to *The Essential C.D. Wright*

Uncollected Poems, Translations & Drafts

5   Why Don't You Go Sit Under a Big Tree

6   Against the Encroaching Greys

8   Like Some Dislocation of Reality

9   Unconditional Love Song

10   Abandon Yourself to That Which Is Inevitable

12   One night last summer

13   The Same Water Everywhere

15   Like the Circles Under Your Eyes

17   her disquietude absorbed.

19   Oblique Gaze

20   Rains

21   Sculptor and Model

22   Voices That Never Arrive

23   Selected translations of an abecedarian

Alla Breve Loving (1976)

27   Posing Without Glasses

28	Poem Before Breakfast
29	Margaret Kaelin Vittitow
30	Alla Breve Loving

Room Rented by a Single Woman (1977)

| 33 | Amnesiac |

Terrorism (1979)

37	Obedience of the Corpse
38	The night before the sentence is carried out
39	Tours

Translations of the Gospel Back into Tongues (1982)

43	Foretold
44	Falling Beasts
46	Libretto
47	Clockmaker with Bad Eyes

Further Adventures with You (1986)

51	Wages of Love
53	Scratch Music
55	This Couple
56	Two Hearts in a Forest
58	Further Adventures with You

String Light (1991)

| 63 | Remarks on Color |
| 65 | Our Dust |

68	What No One Could Have Told Them
71	Detail from *What No One Could Have Told Them*
72	Living

Just Whistle: a valentine (1993)

77	A Brief and Blameless Outline of the Ontogeny of Crow
78	"Because conditions are ideal for crowing"
79	On the Eve of Their Mutually Assured Destruction:
80	Voice of the Ridge

Tremble (1996)

83	Approximately Forever
84	Because Fulfillment Awaits
85	Oneness
87	What Keeps
88	Key Episodes from an Earthly Life
90	In a Piercing and Sucking Species
91	Crescent
92	Everything Good Between Men and Women
93	Morning Star
94	Flame

Deepstep Come Shining (1998)

Cooling Time: An American Poetry Vigil (2005)

| 115 | *from* Op-Ed |
| 117 | *from* Concerning Complexity |

118   *from* Just Looking:

119   *from* Collaborating

121   *from* Five of Us Drove to Horatio:

122   Poetry and Parenting

123   This Much I Know:

124   in our only time.

One Big Self: An Investigation (2003; 2007)

Rising, Falling, Hovering (2008)

145   Re: Happiness, in pursuit thereof

146   *from* Rising, Falling, Hovering

156   End Thoughts

One With Others [a little book of her days] (2010)

The Poet, the Lion, Talking Pictures, El Farolito, a Wedding in St. Roch, the Big Box Store, the Warp in the Mirror, Spring, Midnights, Fire & All (2016)

183   In a Word, a World

184   My American Scrawl

185   "Poems are my building projects"

186   In a Word, a World

187   In a Word, a World

188   The not knowing whether what you've set down is any good

189   In a Word, a World

190   My American Scrawl

191   In a Word, a World

192   In a Word, a World

193	In a Word, a World
194	Questionnaire in January
201	End Sheet

ShallCross (2016)

205	Light Bulb Poem
206	Amarillo Poem
207	Poem with Some Water Damage
208	Poem with a Dead Tree
209	Poem from the End of Old Wire Road
210	Breathtaken
227	Obscurity and Empathy
229	Imaginary Suitcase
230	ShallCross

Casting Deep Shade: An Amble Inscribed to Beech Trees & Co. (2019)

| 257 | Why Leave You So Soon Gone |

259	*Index of Titles*
262	*Acknowledgments*
263	*About the Author*
264	*About the Editors*

Editor's Note

On a wall in Whitechapel I saw it written:
I propose to keep looking. *I propose*
we all keep looking. I propose
it is an unyielding imperative for the poet to do so.

In compiling *The Essential C.D. Wright,* Forrest Gander and I decided to resist simply duplicating the early work represented in her Selected volume, *Steal Away,* and focus more on out-of-print poems, longer excerpts, and previously unpublished works, while still drawing from each of C.D.'s books. It is an almost entirely subjective endeavor, choosing from a poet's corpus whose entirety we believe to be "essential." Forrest and I have revisited her early (and hard-to-find) books from Lost Roads Publishers, have combed through her books from the years she bounced between small presses, working together with a shared goal of highlighting and safeguarding her writing for new generations of readers, while also providing an enticing sampler for those readers who already *know.* Over the coming years, we hope to celebrate her complete writing life in additional volumes. C.D.'s is one of the most distinctive and influential voices of the last fifty years. Her writing is essential to American literature.

C.D. Wright has also been integral to the health and history of Copper Canyon Press, and her writing has been transformative to the identity of the Press, beginning with the publication of *Deepstep Come Shining.* She helped move the Press's aesthetic toward new and diverse territories. The daughter of a judge and a court reporter, she gave a singular voice to moral outrage and poetic provocation and leaned heavily into calling for justice and affirming the overlooked and underserved. C.D. Wright long advocated for the creation within poetry of a modern equivalent of the Federal Writers' Project of the

Works Progress Administration. Like the writers of that era—including Muriel Rukeyser, Richard Wright, Nelson Algren, John Steinbeck, Claude McKay, Zora Neale Hurston, and May Swenson—she wrote about race, class, place, sexuality, and human rights.

I remember once coming home, in the days of answering machines, to discover that C.D. had accidentally called my number, thinking she had reached a policeman from Forrest City, Arkansas. She left on my machine a bunch of polite questions, for an officer who was part of the team that detained a group of Black children in a drained swimming pool. This was part of her research for her book *One With Others [a little book of her days]*, which would win the National Book Critics Circle Award. As with her book about the Louisiana prison industry, *One Big Self*, much of her writing investigated society and the self within society. C.D. was among the first to create what is now considered "docupoetics," an investigative lyric well suited to exposing injustice and degradation. And although her writing in the investigative vein laid the groundwork for socially minded and transformational books, her passion went beyond moral urgency: she held a deep and abiding love for the vehicle of the word—"I love them all." Her dedication in pursuit of a project was indefatigable. Once, when she was asked to write about a favorite tree, her love letter grew to a 250-page exaltation of the beech. She played with words, she teased them, raged at and with them, and she let words live in the ears and mouths of others, always envisioning "A Reader for Every Writer":

> I am privileged to talk to people almost every
> day who read deeply and widely, and when I step
> outside of that special circle, I can get an instant
> case of the willies, but am propelled in another
> instant to interact, to attune to the copious
> dimensions of living. The call of the writer is the
> same as the call of the reader. Take me to other
> planes of myself.

Over my thirty years of working as her editor, C.D. and her poems have taken me to "other planes of myself," and her writing remains one of my great loves

xiv

in the American literary landscape. C.D. Wright came shining as one big self, a writer who was one with others and is undeniably essential. As a reviewer noted in *The New York Times,* she "belongs to a school of exactly one."

MICHAEL WIEGERS

A Tiny Introduction to *The Essential C.D. Wright*

Since she was raised in the house of a court reporter and a judge whose idol was Abraham Lincoln, it may not seem a stretch that C.D.'s constitution was ethical to the core. She never modified her innate sense of right and wrong to let something pass in a social situation—but that didn't mean she was pious. One of her most immediately apparent qualities, in argument or casual conversation, was her quick sense of humor. The essential C.D. was a woman who would speak her mind, her blue-grey eyes sparking, with an unrehearsed, unpretentious directness so rare it was disarming. And she wasn't afraid of anyone. (I remember her, across the dinner table, contradicting Susan Sontag minutes after they'd been introduced; something to do with the history of Russian film, I think, which I hadn't been aware C.D. knew much about.)

I mention C.D.'s ethical orientation from the start not as encomium but because we see the same orientation in her books. All of them. *One With Others* and *One Big Self,* each composed—like Indra's net—as linked sequences so interconnected they can't be wholly represented in excerpt, are most obviously focused on dignity, justice, and intersubjective responsibility. Not of course as philosophy or polemic; as poetry. But even when we look back to her early poems, "Obedience of the Corpse" or "Tours," for example, we see struggle and innocence, ethical gestures of tenderness and care in a world of brutalities.

C.D.'s work is so quirky—mixing rural Arkansas vernacular and landscape references with a sophisticated intellectual bent and an exuberance for lexical particularity—that it is surely among the most difficult poetries to translate. And yet her books in translation became popular in Sweden, Norway, China, Mexico, Brazil, Spain, Slovenia, and Argentina. Since her death, conferences and prizes have been named in her honor. There's the $45,000 annual C.D. Wright Award for Poetry from the Foundation for Contemporary Arts, the C.D. Wright/Academy of American Poets Prize, the Arkansas International C.D. Wright Prize for Poetry, the C.D. Wright Women Writers Conference, the annual C.D. Wright Lecture Series at Brown University, etc. Her biography is forthcoming, along with a book of critical essays on her work. This kind of ample and ongoing admiration is, I think you know, extremely unusual. Perhaps

xvii

unprecedented. And it speaks more clearly than I can of the lasting power of her work and the vast numbers of readers that her writing touched, and touched deeply.

For thirty-five years, we lived together. In all that time, I can say with utter honesty, she was not for one minute uninteresting. Or uninterested. She was, she is, the most fascinating person I will ever have known. Her passions were extensive and ever expanding. She was given to lake swimming and hiking. To trees and plants that she would casually name as she passed them—the Latin names and common ones. She fell in love with Mexico. She was a distracted driver except in New York City, where she woke up and outhustled the taxis. She was irrevocably devoted to our child, Brecht. She was committedly amorous. She poured herself into friendships and somehow invented time to intensify them. She took her role as a professor seriously, was unflattering and honest with her students. And when others bowed out, she reluctantly took on more and more at work. I know that, many times, she pulled the load for me. But it wasn't until after her death, as I collected her folders and heard from friends and strangers, that I realized quite how vastly she gave herself to others. I thought I knew, but I didn't. She was constantly advocating, taking the initiative, championing those who would never even know how she had acted on their behalf. And somehow, she wrote her books.

Michael Wiegers and I have selected poems from most of C.D.'s books of poetry, a body of work I know by heart. It was especially difficult to excerpt from the sui generis book-length projects: *One With Others, One Big Self,* and *Casting Deep Shade: An Amble Inscribed to Beech Trees & Co.* Although those books really need to be read whole, perhaps these excerpts will inspire new readers to seek them out. Here, in any case, are many of the poems I know she considered durable, poems I remember reading in drafts, poems I heard her recite in public. It took C.D. a long while to find a publisher as committed to her as she was to her writing. She found that publisher and a subsequent friendship with its editor, Michael Wiegers, at Copper Canyon Press. I am ever grateful to him, to them. To her.

FORREST GANDER

THE ESSENTIAL C.D. WRIGHT

Uncollected Poems, Translations & Drafts

Why Don't You Go Sit Under a Big Tree

While you're at it
Well a great many things have been said in the last few minutes
and precious little taken back
Well we've not been shaken out of magnolias
Well tomorrow will be a hard day as they say but we will have
B's birthday party and we will have music
I am not missing any fingers or toes
Well I think I will go up and talk to Anise
The fields on the north side of town have big houses on them now
The root cellar filled up with water,

along with white pianos and floral furniture

This may be the only snapshot I have for which you did not pose

I see him walking down the hall and I say B

we've been worried about you
I don't think he realizes the effect his appearance has

Put it all down anyway
And you know what he says to me
Here you go baby my shroud es su shroud

Ginger roots—for the dark thoughts
Dying this way it is nothing it's a breeze a snap
is like losing a sock

Nonresistance to evil—montezuma in face of imprisonment by cortez (prescott)
Irrigate with blood
Andante ladies take it easy
Ineluctably over

The goose buried up to its neck to make her pâté—
Preamble to war

Against the Encroaching Greys

I held up the femur
of a grasshopper

some blue air fell over me
what I want is less clear to me
now than it was then

to be loved to the end
without ruth or recrimination
to forgive myself as others

have forgiven me
to enjoy the birds
with little bones

at the farmers' market
I still see his truck
from time to time

notices on utility poles
for a lost dog answering
to Scout sometimes I sit

in a cafe pretending
to read but knowing

I want to be the one
to find Scout
instead

I do what I have done
I wake up and join
the struggle

of the trees
to find a way
through and then

a dark clot
of poetry breaks off

Like Some Dislocation of Reality

Clothes laid out behind her on the bed as if they were going out

A table, as if someone fiercely hungry were coming
or just someone fierce

The kitten that survived under the stairs slept on his sweater

Without food or water or company

One of the many things she neglected to ask

If he would bring her something sweet when he returned

How this feels: diminished by one, it hasn't got a name

You don't get it, she discovered among his crumpled juvenilia,
I was never here

Unconditional Love Song

Later she would remember it started to pour

the storm blew everything out

before the coffee finished its brew

and she could finish reading a report

on some boys holed up in a derelict house

after stoning a swan to death

she wrapped her head in a towel

and sat down by the open window

even though the sound of the river was not there

the memory of the sound was

even though her husband did not appear in the door

talking to her about the day ahead

the day ahead was there

Abandon Yourself to That Which Is Inevitable

       Opposite the parking lot,
demolition rubble, and beyond it the garden of a neglected estate. The relict
lay reading.

The great nothing was there. Always.
Listen, Trespasser.

A bird half convinces her she is hearing more than one line at once. Smell of
dog, no, drunkard's urine on the wrought iron. A button and a condom on the walk.
The relict lay reading in the yarrow, the red clover, the spent lilies. The blue spruce
toppling itself; one of the oaks dispersed in chunks. Rivulets threading her
personal hill

where the relict lay reading in the spent lilies of the valley and
the tall candles of mullein that took over once the keepers were let go.
A pergola struggling to support its vine. All but aloud it struggles. The blue
spruce leaning; loyal oak in chunks. A trench
part-dug to reroute the runoff.

Rock at every strike
of the pick.

The relict cursing the contractor's bad fill. Cursing the contractor's grass.
Her smoke bush cleared the winter, and the spring, but Robert didn't.

The relict lay reading in the contractor's bad grass. I used to breathe sleep eat poetry.
Until could not see to read except the large-print books, mysteries, tell-alls, and
how to build waterfalls, but could see the hollows in the small of his buttocks,
the fair hair feathering into his pitchy seam.

I could see rings of brilliance
beyond any visible human means.

The relict lay reading below a house so large it could rain in front with no
cloud in sight around back. Unseasonable sadness of unseen sprinklers.
Reverberation of nonstop traffic
on Reading Road.

It doesn't look a bit peaceful
out there. Pointing past the trespasser.

Standing on her personal hill. Her dress fluttering in the absence of the
weakest wind. Exposing the loose flesh below the arm commonly called bat wings.

Just. Could
somebody
please
tell me.
What did it mean
that I was a girl.

One night last summer

a vagrant scent woke her though it soon melted
into the trees. She had been dreaming of
reading the paper in a foreign country. Words filtered
through her haltingly since she did not really know
the language; thoughts, mothlike, fluttered but didn't
distinguish themselves. She felt that she had been
on this road before. She felt hesitant to
continue. It ended abruptly at a small pond
in an unkempt garden. The light revived her—primordial
as if witness to the collision of debris that created the moon.

She pulled her ears back to listen.

The Same Water Everywhere

Party of one
at the Black Hawk.

Writing into the night.

From Rock River, fish
on a platter.

Part of a glove
rotting in the mud.

Shot off a fence, the tin
can in the timothy.

She fired once. Once:

talked into a tape recorder.

The young poplars shushed
then loquacious again.

15 below. She goes
to her mailbox.

Her mineral tranquility.

Chicory and campion in summer;
some steps will want repair.

Daubs of tar near the shed
where a boat there was.

Al's left hand decomposed
not far from the source

of the river

into which hers also pours.

At the picture window her friend
Sun squints for a little while.

Where she sat long
in a yellow cable sweater.

Writing into the light.

I like to think
the snow in her low boots

is boiling
on my stove.

Scratch *yellow.*

homage to LN with T&G

Like the Circles Under Your Eyes

clouds jammed into the foreground   big toe in the suckhole

with all our know-how   all our equipment   you would think

we would be on guard   be smarter than water   less indifferent

than the critter at the corner   or the machine   that rolled over its head

so early in the season   so many dead things to build on

a broom goes before me   the dog refuses to budge

leaves winging down onto leaves   under such conditions

on american soil   longtime dealers in old things unemployed

shrink   teachers   pastry chefs   horn player with a monster sound

the stuff of legends   married cousins   then a loopy face

behind a glass enclosure   being driven away   sliding from sight

a man smokes listlessly on a bed   next to a mound

of swollen books   written in french   his shoes set out to dry

scent of last tenant   unwashed socks shut up in a box   crept out

onto the landing   of the photographer's house   searched

9/11 by the authorities   sprayed that hateful date on the front

windows tall enough for a mast to pass under   my friend

didn't lose much   by comparison   but still   the top floor on top of which   mother murdered   husband deserted

who kept hens in the heart of town   where I used to hear birds

when I phoned   now bullhorn now chopper   someone

puts a plate in her hands   hours later   someone takes the plate

from her lap   and says damn if it isn't overcast again   it's time to get out

the candlesticks

for DL

her disquietude absorbed.

By an attendant memory   she is walking

alongside the child on his cycle

obeying the familiar path that curves toward

the gaslit entrance before reaching

the broken birdbath and the markers

of Blythe, Horsfall, and Potter

whose stone is hard to read

for the gargantuan hydrangea.

   Dispelled

by a continuous shuttling back and forth

downstairs   sound of water being drawn.

Wet-headed;

seated   on a metal chair

holding an extension cord

her clothes swarm the floor.

Be the shoulders dusted as shoulders can glare

commotion of morning grows   insistent.

Be the credits opened boldly.

Be the air expanding at supersonic speed.

Be the windows let up and the centenarian tree dependably there; be

Oblique Gaze

by Marcelo Uribe

translated with Marcelo Hernandez Castillo

These are the lines of your face,
the angle of your gaze.
This is how your voice is written
In those pupils, with these strokes,
the words that lead
your memory astray,
the unfocused light that filters the air.

The eyes pause, move on, return;
looking for evidence of you among the shapes.

But you are only cloth
with pigments attached,
a memory of air,
only a way to see and touch,
a name on a slip of paper,
a memory on a gravestone
that sooner or later
no one will be able to read.

Rains

by Marcelo Uribe

translated with Marcelo Hernandez Castillo

May the whitening sky
and the black clouds
wash the darkness from this
and every night.
Let this water carry
all waters
and may it be all the rivers;
let it take over
so the eyes become water
and water becomes pain
and everything be erased
by water;
let it rain on the light
and the wind
and let wind and light
be water that disappears;
that for forty nights
the rain may not cease
until everything becomes rain;
let it not be water,
river of memory
that vanishes but doesn't end.

for Vicente Rojo

Sculptor and Model

by Marcelo Uribe

translated with Marcelo Hernandez Castillo

Nothing you can observe will preserve her profile,
you leave your decrepit trace on everything.
And if you last, it will be for your gift of fire
that never fails,
because you don't exist in the space where you're molded
nor in your handwriting over the water
that wipes the ash off a dream.
I can only reach you, only touch, only caress you
in your immaculate art of disappearance.

Voices That Never Arrive

by Marcelo Uribe

translated with Marcelo Hernandez Castillo

It takes the dawn
rummaging through the sky.
It takes its uncertainty
like words
that never return,
like the voices
that never arrive
from imaginary memories.
—You come
because you know
I am going to die.

It is better if the morning
we hoped for
doesn't come,
and in this moment
everything would shine
forever.

Selected translations of an abecedarian

by Paol Keineg

A

At the left, the ax; at the right, the saw.
The ax in the block, the saw on the sawhorse.
Sawdust smothers the walk. Sitting in the
shed to watch the rain come down. Some opposition
before the whole picture dissolves into nothingness.
Threatened later by the willingness to believe
it there. Reading time in the shed, rhythmic
fall of the ax in the block. Several things:
teeth of the saw pressed into the palm, the
string you twist by rotating the lathe, the piercing
blue teeth. Capable of taking off in plain view,
behind the dirty panes, the pylon and its supports,
big field of potatoes, by succeeding fragments,
by counterweights, the voice, the place, the
vibrations, dilution, clockwise.

D

Down from the web in the thorns glides a spider
with fur the color of weeds. Here I am. Desire
to please to which one adds desire to die. All
that comes from above makes things obscure.
All that, obscure, is tied up in a motion which
wrenches the heart. To take it is to pervert
it. This is why the entire poem is for another
day. I have not taken hold: the wild broom
flames near the telephone booth, a woman
talks crushing the receiver against her ear,

I remain incapable of high thought. To grow
old does not snuff out the scruples.

G

Great guys of the future, we have learned
that the chiliagon has a thousand sides, and
you whose starlight is not burdened by a bestiary,
you take the chances of the practical and
modern life. From here to the sea, there's
the moor, with the horrors of the dream and
the dim explanatory rays. On the coast a thousand
eyes are trained on the arrival of the first
light: the destruction of a people, more the
assent to destruction. Apart from adventures
of reason that open on the void, let us hold
onto signs of distress, instants of folly. Guys,
great guys, thus as we had read, the myriagon
is a polygon whose sides cannot be imagined.

H

Hash, hasher. Seated, to seat. Ah yes, ah evening.
One should take advantage of it. Summer
evening on the darkening page; the scream
of a pig whose throat is slit. On the square,
light still, Page, Pope, and King bowl for wine.
Who knows who keeps silent behind the flickering
walls. For a long time already some partial
truths have abandoned the dining rooms: let's
cry, my friends. Let's have a hard, hard cry
and wave our big wet hankies. Let's run, my
friends, behind the balls which soar and explode.

Alla Breve Loving

MILL MOUNTAIN PRESS, 1976

Posing Without Glasses

This is Carolyn standing
Before an unpainted shed

The grass is high and wet
Against her legs
A fan of red roses
Bars the rotting door

Her left hand covers one eye
As if it had been pecked

Yet her skin
It smells of mint
Her free hand is full of dimes
The trill of a flute lights her breasts

Poem Before Breakfast

She pulled the sundress over her head
Forgetting her pants, her sandals,
And her ring;

Leaving her glasses on the sink
She unlatched the screen.

With her lunch money
Tucked in her pocket;
Her clean manila hair
Settling down her back.

She went out on her toes
To see if the painted bunting
Had fled her wedding bush.

Margaret Kaelin Vittitow

Wanted herself to be
A sundial a tiger a surgeon
A penguin a fighter a whiteowl
"None of that for girls, now girl"

Wanted to be
Pummeling rocks
Clogging on a bridge
Smashing old toys
Belting out tunes
In a cowboy saloon

And instead
Settled into a box with a man
Who fixed clocks fixed clocks
Fixed clocks

Alla Breve Loving

Three people drinking out of the bottle
in the living room.
A cold rain. Quiet as a mirror.

One of the men
stuffs his handkerchief in his coat,
climbs the stairs with the girl.
The other man is left sitting

at the desk with the wine and the headache,
turning an old Ellington side
over in his mind. And over.

He held her like a saxophone
when she was his girl.
Her tongue trembling at the reed.

The man lying next to her now
thinks of another woman.
Her white breath idling

before he drove off.
He said something about a spell,
watching the snow fall on her shoulders.

The musician
crawls back into his horn,
ancient terrapin
at the approach of the wheel.

Room Rented by a Single Woman

LOST ROADS PUBLISHERS, 1977

Amnesiac

for Sonnyman, third cousin, disappeared
eighteen years ago

We cleared the table for cards
when the power came back on
The man stood outside the door
combing water through his hair
Forgive me he said
I think I've come far
and lost my calling
After that he drew three jacks
After that he worked harder than a Shaker
though he seemed to sleep always
never going to bed
We found the Lincoln in the reservoir
the plates rusted off
The man said it's a shame
and headed the tractor home
When he realized he could tune the upright
he went up the loft
with the View-Master
He held it to the moon
The reel he liked to look at is A Visit to Taj Mahal

Terrorism

LOST ROADS PUBLISHERS, 1979

Obedience of the Corpse

The midwife puts a rag in the dead woman's hand,
takes the hairpins out.

She smells apples,
wonders where she keeps them in the house.
Nothing is under the sink
but a broken sack of potatoes growing eyes.

She hopes the mother's milk is good awhile longer,
the woman up the road is still nursing.
She remembers the neighbor
and the dead woman never got along.

A limb breaks.
She knows it's not the wind.
Somebody needs to set out some poison.

She looks to see if the woman wrote down any names,
finds a white shirt to wrap the baby in.
It's beautiful she thinks—
snow nobody has walked on.

The night before the sentence is carried out

                                a woman is riding a bus
with a sack of black apples in her lap.

The bus stalls on the dam.
She pulls a knife out of the sack, throws it
in the water with the blade half-open

like the eyes of a lawyer
who has been drinking heavy
for a month. More than a month.

He passes out in his boat.
When he comes to, the lake is another man's
suit, in the billfold
photo of another man's wife.

The woman waits for everyone to get off
before she does.
She reaches up to put the pins in her hair.

The condemned man is rubbing his arms
thinking about someone
he used to be married to.
He reaches under the cot, touches the cold wire.

She stands up brushing her clothes,
the bottom falls out of the sack.
She leaves the apples scattered in the aisle.

Tours

A girl on the stairs listens to her father
beat up her mother.
Doors bang.
She comes down in her nightgown.

The piano stands there in the dark
like a boy with an orchid.

She plays what she can
then she turns the lamp on.

Her mother's music is spread out
on the floor like brochures.

She hears her father
running through the leaves.

The last black key
she presses stays down, makes no sound,
like someone putting their tongue where their tooth had been.

Translations of the Gospel Back into Tongues

STATE UNIVERSITY OF NEW YORK PRESS, 1982

Foretold

Even in countries with the blackest eyes
Those with one blue one rule.
The bad doctor is respected, the well-witcher is not.
This is the dog's life.

With daylight
The called climb out of the hills under darkening
Loads. They lay their burdens down
Of an evening, snore like the wind.
Asleep, they know themselves
As the ones who fly.

To set foot on the desired land
All incurable dreamers must rise and go down
To the thirty-fifth latitude.

Approach the wide porches of the chosen
With ears laid back,
In accordance with the common law—
The baddest dog entitled one bite,
And as it has been written
Is better to die trying than not to die.

Falling Beasts

Girls marry young
In towns in the mountains.
They're sent to the garden
For beets. They come to the table
With their hair gleaming,
Their breath missing.
In my book love is darker
Than cola. It can burn
A hole clean through you.
When the first satellite
Flew over, men stood
On their property, warm
Even in their undershirts,
Longing to shoot something.
The mule looks down
The barrel of the gun,
Another long row to plow.
Bills pile up in fall
Like letters from a son
In the army. An explosion
Kills a quiet man.
Another sits beside a brass lamp
In a white shirt
And cancels his pay.
A thousand dulcimers are carved
By the one called Double Thumb.
Winter cuts us down
Like a coach. Spits snow.
Horses flinch
Against the cold spurs in the sky.
We look for the oak
Who loves our company

More than other oaks.
The loveliest beds
Are left undone.
Hope is a pillow
Hold on.

Libretto

Night is dark
on the streets without names.

Men piss in the ditch, on the toe of their shoes
thinking it must be rain or hail.

The feet of their women swell like a melon.
Their ironing boards bow
under the weight of beautiful linen
they do for other women.

Radios are turned up to beat thunder,
translations of the gospel
back into tongues.

The tiger lilies' tremble.
Bottles busted, somebody cut.

A man in a black shirt
gets off the bus with no suitcase,
leans on his wife. Umbrella
with a broken spoke.

A girl sits out-of-doors in her slip.
She turns fourteen, twenty-eight, fifty-six,
goes crazy.

The saxophone plays it for somebody else.
Play hell.

Clockmaker with Bad Eyes

I close the shop at six. Welcome wind,
weekend with two suns, night with a travel book,
the dog-eared sheets of a bed
I will not see again.

I not of time, lost in time
learned from watches—
a second is a killing thing.

Live your life. Your eyes go. Take your body
out for walks along the waters
of a cold and loco planet.

Love whatever flows. Cooking smoke, woman's blood,
tears. Do you hear what I'm telling you?

Further Adventures with You

CARNEGIE MELLON UNIVERSITY PRESS, 1986

Wages of Love

The house is watched, the watchers only planets.

Very near the lilac
                    a woman leaves her night soil
to be stepped in. Like other animals.
                    Steam lifts off her mess.

They have power, but not water.
                    Pregnant. She must be.

The world is all that is the case.

You can hear the strike of the broom, a fan
                    slicing overhead light.
At the table the woman stares at a dish
                    of peaches, plums; black ants
filing down the sill to bear away the fly.

Everywhere in America is summer. The young
                    unaware they are young, their minds
on other wounds or the new music.

The heart some bruised fruit
knocked loose by a long stick
                    aches at the stem.
It's not forbidden to fall out of love
                    like from a tree.

As for the tenants whose waters
                    will break in this bed,
may they live through the great pain;
may their offspring change everything—

                    because everything must change.

The man joins the woman in the kitchen. They touch
the soft place of their fruit.
They enter in, tell their side, and pass through.

Scratch Music

How many threads have I broken with my teeth. How many times
have I looked at the stars and felt ill. Time here is divided into before
and since your shuttering in 1978. I remember hanging on to the
hood of the big-fendered Olds with a mess of money in my purse.
Call that romance. Some memory precedes you: when I wanted
lederhosen because I'd read *Heidi.* And how I wanted my folks to
build a fallout shelter so I could arrange the cans. And coveting
Mother's muskrat. I remember college. And being in VISTA: I asked
the librarian in Banks, the state's tomato capital, if she had any black
literature and she said they used to have *Little Black Sambo* but the white
children tore out pages and wrote ugly words inside. Someone said
if I didn't like Banks I should go to Moscow. I said, Come on, let's go
outside and shoot the hoop. I've got a jones to beat your butt. I haven't
changed. Now if I think of the earth's origins, I get vertigo. When I
think of its death, I fall. I've picked up a few things. I know if you
want songbirds, plant berry trees. If you don't want birds, buy a
rubber snake. I remember that town with the Alcoa plant I toured.
The manager kept referring to the workers as Alcoans. I thought of
hundreds of flexible metal beings bent over assemblages. They
sparked. What would I do in Moscow. I have these dreams—relatives
loom over my bed. We should put her to sleep, Lonnie says. Go home
old girl, go home, my aunt says. Why should I go home before her I
want to say. But I am bereft. So how is life in the other world. Do
you get the news. Are you allowed a pet. But I wanted to show you
how I've grown, what I know: I keep my bees far from the stable,
they can't stand how horses smell. And I know sooner or later an old
house will need a new roof. And more than six years have whistled
by since you blew your heart out like the porchlight. Reason and
meaning don't step into another lit spot like a well-meaning stranger
with a hat. And mother's mother, who has lived in the same house
ten-times-six years, told me, We didn't know we had termites until
they swarmed. Then we had to pull up the whole floor. "Too late, no

more . . . ," you know the poem. But you, you bastard. You picked up a
gun in winter as if it were a hat and you were leaving a restaurant:
full, weary, and thankful to be spending the evening with no one.

This Couple

Now is when we love to sit before mirrors
with a dark beer or hand out leaflets
at chain-link gates or come together after work
listening to each other's hard day. The engine dies,
no one hurries to go in. We might
walk around in the yard not making a plan.
The freeway is heard but there's no stopping
progress, and the week has barely begun. Then
we are dressed. It rains. Our heads rest
against the elevator wall inhaling a stranger;
we think of cliffs we went off
with our laughing friends. The faces
we put our lips to. Our wonderful sex
under whatever we wear. And of the car
burning on the side of the highway. Jukeboxes
we fed. Quarters circulating with our prints.
Things we sent away for. Long drives. The rain. Cafes
where we ate late and once only. Eyes of an animal
in the headlamps. The guest books that verify
our whereabouts. Your apple core in the ashtray.
The pay toilets where we sat without paper. Rain.
Articles left with ex-lovers. The famous
ravine of childhood. Movie lines we've stood in
when it really came down. Moments
we have felt forsaken waiting for the others
to step from the wrought-iron compartment,
or passing through some town with the dial
on a Mexican station, wondering for the life of us,
where are we going and when would we meet.

Two Hearts in a Forest

Evening Shade

I am over here, by the tomato cages
gently touching the wire,
watching one lightning bug light another
freshly fucked and childless
an astonished woman in a wedding gown
who can see in the dark, almost.

Lush Life

I could have gone to Stringtown
O I could have wasted away
moaning in the swamped bed
among winged roaches and twisted figs
between the fern and dark thighs.

Hotel Philharmonic

We have arrived drunk, jobless,
brilliant with love.
Music commences:
You hold out your glass
I lift my dress. My hands
saved like candles for a storm
in yours. We fall
through the night's caesura.

Lost Roads

As though following a series of clues, we drove
through this ragged range, a town of magnetic springs

our arms in the window, browning.
The sun was torching the hair of maples.
You didn't sing in key, you sang
"Famous Blue Raincoat."
I had a dream, Life isn't real.
Already the sad rapture entering.

Mountain Herald

This time, the Celebrant vowed, No one would intinct,
blowing the unsteady flames of our face.
We rose and married well, my nose
in your tender swarthiness. I'll never forget
the whirling floor, the bassman's royal head.
As for the uninvited they were asked in.
Melon, not cake was served;
there was japonica and spirea. Still
they were a little late for the forsythia.
God yes, the forsythia, the forsythia.

Further Adventures with You

We are on a primeval river in a reptilian den.

There are birds you don't want to tangle with, trees
        you cannot identify . . .

        Somehow we spend the evening with Mingus
in a White Castle. Or somewhere. Nearly drunk. He says
        he would like to play for the gang.

        All of us ride to Grandmother Wright's house
in a van. It's her old neighborhood. I think we look
like a carton of colas sitting up stiffly
        behind the glass.

        She is recently dead. Some of her belongings
are gone. Her feather mattress has been rolled back
from the springs. It turns out Mingus has forgotten
his cello. We lie on our sides in jackets and jeans
        as if it were a beach in fall.

        Then it is Other Mama's house. She is
recently dead. We stretch out on Other Mama's carpet
        pulling at its nap.

You and I have stomped into A-Mart to buy papers
and schnapps. Two boys, one pimply, the other clear-skinned,
        blow in with blue handkerchiefs
and a gun. Blue is the one color I notice tonight.
        They tell us, Take off.

We're gone. We're on the back of the bus with the liquor.
        The silly boys have shot the package-store clerk.
We're the only suspects. You have a record so you're in a sweat.
You're flashing black, white. Around the nose and mouth

you remind me a little of Sam Cooke. I think
he was shot in a motel. A case of sexual madness. We get off
at an old bar that shares a wall with a school for girls.

The police collar us there. They separate us for questioning.
You show a work card that claims you're a male dancer.
You pull out a gun. Where did you get that. And you blast them.
It's their hearts, I think, My God.

You yell out a nonword and hit the doors. I run
through the back. It's the girls' school. They seem to be
getting ready for a revue. I try to blend in—hoist a mattress,
somebody's music up a staircase. There are racks
of costumes on wheels, flats of moving scenery . . .

There is the river, the horrible featherless bird. The tree,
not a true palm but of the palm family.

String Light

UNIVERSITY OF GEORGIA PRESS, 1991

Remarks on Color

1. highway patched with blacktop, service station at the crossroads
2. cream soda in the popbox, man sitting on the popbox
3. a fully grown man
4. filthy toilets, just hold it a little while longer
5. shacks ringed with daylilies, then a columned house in shade
6. condensation off soybeans
7. someone known as Skeeter
8. his whole life
9. flatbed loaded with striped melons
10. Lopez's white car at JB's mother's house
11. katydids crepitating in the tall grass
12. gar wrapping itself in your line
13. gourds strung between poles
14. imagine a tribe of color-blind people, and there could easily be one,
    they would not have the same color concepts as we do
15. that's trumpet vine; that's what we call potato vine
16. no potatoes come of it though
17. no potatoes I know
18. I come back here about three years ago to see if I could eke out a
    living then I run on to Rhonda
19. help me Rhonda help help me Rhonda
20. E-Z on E-Z off
21. out of wedlock, wedlocked
22. planks nailed across kitchen doorway for a bar; living room turned
    into dance floor
23. drinking canned heat
24. the shit can make you permanently blind
25. sizzling nights
26. what do you suppose became of Fontella Bass
27. get your own sound then notes go with your sound—it's like a color,
    my color—I'm black brown with a little red-orange in my skin
28. red looks good on me

29. and yet we could imagine circumstances under which we would say, these
    people see other colors in addition to ours
30. what the Swede concluded: if you want to know what's the matter with blacks
    in America study the other side of the color line
31. I am just telling you what the man figured out
32. there is, after all, no commonly accepted criterion for what is a color unless it is
    one of our colors
33. check this:
34. at the time of his death Presley's was the second most reproduced image in
    the world
35. the first was Mickey Mouse
36. Lansky Brothers—down on Beale—outfitted the johns of Memphis
37. and Elvis
38. R-U ready for Jesus R-U packed up
39. just don't compare me to any white musicians
40. take me witcha man when you go

Our Dust

I am your ancestor. You know next to nothing
about me.
There is no reason for you to imagine
the rooms I occupied or my heavy hair.
Not the faint vinegar smell of me. Or
the rubbered damp
of Forrest and I coupling on the landing
en route to our detached day.

You didn't know my weariness, error, incapacity.
I was the poet
of shadow work and towns with quarter-inch
phone books, of failed
roadside zoos. The poet of yard eggs and
sharpening shops,
jobs at the weapons plant and the Maybelline
factory on the penitentiary road.

A poet of spiderwort and jacks-in-the-pulpit,
hollyhocks against the toolshed.
An unsmiling dark blond.
The one with the trowel in her handbag.
I dug up protected and private things.
That sort, I was.
My graves went undecorated and my churches
abandoned. This wasn't planned, but practice.

I was the poet of short-tailed cats and yellow
line paint.
Of satellite dishes and Peterbilt trucks. Red Man
Chewing Tobacco, Triple Hit
Creme Soda. Also of dirt daubers, nightcrawlers,

martin houses, honey, and whetstones
from the Novaculite Uplift.

I had registered dogs 4 sale; rocks, dung
and straw.
I was a poet of hummingbird hives along with
redheaded stepbrothers.

The poet of good walking shoes—a necessity
in vernacular parts—and push mowers.
The rumor that I was once seen sleeping
in a refrigerator box is false (he was a brother
who hated me).
Nor was I the one lunching at the Governor's
Mansion.

I didn't work off a grid. Or prime the surface
if I could get off without it. I made
simple music
out of sticks and string. On side B of me,
experimental guitar, night repairs, and suppers
such as this.
You could count on me to make a bad situation
worse like putting liquid makeup over
a passion mark.

I never raised your rent. Or anyone else's by God.
Never said I loved you. The future gave me chills.
I used the medium to say: Arise arise and
come together.
Free your children. Come on everybody. Let's start
with Baltimore.

Believe me I am not being modest when I
admit my life doesn't bear repeating. I

agreed to be the poet of one life,
one death alone. I have seen myself
in the black car. I have seen the retreat
of the black car.

What No One Could Have Told Them

Once he comes to live on the outside of her, he will not sleep
through the night or the next 400. He sleeps not, they sleep not.
Ergo they steer gradually mad. The dog's head shifts to another
paw under the desk. Over a period of 400 nights.

You will see, she warns him. Life is full of television sets,
invoices, organs of other animals thawing on counters.

In her first dream of him, she leaves him sleeping on Mamo's
salt-bag quilt behind her alma mater. Leaves him to the Golden
Goblins. Sleep, pretty one, sleep.

. . . the quilt that comforted her brother's youthful bed, the
quilt he took to band camp.

Huh oh, he says, Huh oh. His word for many months.
Merrily pouring a bottle of Pledge over the dog's dull coat. And
with a round little belly that shakes like jelly.

Waiting out a shower in the Border Cafe; the bartender
spoons a frozen strawberry into his palm-leaf basket while they
lift their frosted mugs in a grateful click.

He sits up tall in his grandfather's lap, waving and waving to
the Blue Bonnet truck. Bye, blue, bye.

In the next dream he stands on his toes, executes a flawless
flip onto the braided rug. Resprings to crib.

The salt-bag quilt goes everywhere, the one the bitch
Rosemary bore her litters on. The one they wrap around the
mower, and bundle with black oak leaves.

How the bowl of Quick Quaker Oats fits his head.

He will have her milk at 1:42, 3:26, 4 a.m. Again at 6. Bent
over the rail to settle his battling limbs down for an afternoon
nap. Eyes shut, trying to picture what in the world she has on.

His night-light—a snow-white pair of porcelain owls.

They remember him toothless, with one tooth, two tooths,
five or seven scattered around in his head. They can see the day
when he throws open his jaw to display several vicious rows.

Naked in a splash of sun, he pees into a paper plate the guest
set down in the grass as she reached for potato chips.

Suppertime, the dog takes leave of the desk's cool cavity to
patrol his high chair.

How patiently he pulls Kleenex from a box. Tissue by tissue.
How quietly he stands at the door trailing the White Cloud;
swabs his young hair with the toilet brush.

*The dog inherits the salt-bag quilt. The one her Mamo made
when she was seventeen—girlfriends stationed around a frame in black stockings
sewing, talking about things their children would do;*

He says: cereal, byebye, shoe, raisin, nobody. He hums.

She stands before the medicine chest, drawn. Swiftly he
tumps discarded Tampax and hair from an old comb into
her tub.

Wearily the man enters the house through the back. She isn't
dressed. At the table there is weeping. Curses. Forking dried
breasts of chicken.

*while Little Sneed sat on the floor beneath the frame, pushing
the needles back through.*

One yawn followed by another yawn. Then little fists screwing little eyes. The wooden crib stuffed with bears and windup pillows wheeled in to receive him. Out in a twinkle. The powdered bottom airing the dark. The 400th night. When they give up their last honeyed morsel of love; the dog nestles in the batting of the salt-bag quilt commencing its long mope unto death.

Detail from *What No One Could Have Told Them*

Naked in a splash of sun, he pees into a paper plate
the guest set down on the lawn as she reached
naked in a splash of sun into a naked sun splash
He pees naked into a paper plate a plate the guest set down
into a plate of white paper the guest set down He pees
into a plate the guest set down on the lawn in back of the airy house
a paper plate the guest set down He pees on the lawn
He pees into a white paper plate a living fountain of pee
a golden jet of pure baby pee from His seven month old penis
His uncircumcised penis not even one year old a jet
of pure gold into an uncircumcised splash of sun
a beautiful gold arc of pee in a splash of uncircumcised sun
naked in a splash of sun He pees into a paper plate
a white paper plate the guest set down on the airy lawn
in back of the airy white house into a paper white plate
weighted down with baked beans and slabs of spiced ham
the guest set down on the lawn in back of the white house
on the lovely expanse of lawn the guest set down the paper plate
on the lawn as she leaned forward in the canvas sling
of her chair as she reached out of her green sleeve
into a white paper plate the guest set down on the lawn He pees
as she reached out of her green butterfly sleeve
out of the beautiful arc of her iridescent sleeve as she
set down on the expanding lovely lawn a paper plate
He pees naked in a splash of sun as she reached for potato chips.

Living

If this is Wednesday, write Lazartigues, return library books, pick up passport form, cancel the paper.

If this is Wednesday, mail B her flyers and K her shirts. Last thing I asked as I walked K to her car, "You sure you have everything?" "Oh yes," she smiled, as she squalled off. Whole wardrobe in front closet.

Go to Morrison's for paint samples, that's where housepainter has account (near Pier One), swing by Gano St. for another bunch of hydroponic lettuce. Stop at cleaners if there's parking.

Pap smear at 4. After last month with B's ear infections, can't bear sitting in damn doctor's office. Never a magazine or picture on the wall worth looking at. Pack a book.

Ever since B born, nothing comes clear. My mind like a mirror that's been in a fire. Does this happen to the others.

If this is Wednesday, meet Moss at the house at noon. Pick B up first, call sitter about Friday evening. If she prefers, can bring B to her (hope she keeps the apartment warmer this year).

Need coat hooks and picture hangers for office. Should take car in for air filter, oil change. F said one of back tires low. Don't forget car payment, late last two months in a row.

If this is Wednesday, there's a demo on the green at 11. Took B to his first down at Quonset Point in August. Blue skies. Boston collective provided good grub for all. Long column of denims and flannel shirts. Smell of patchouli made me so wistful, wanted to buy a woodstove, prop my feet up, share a J

and a pot of Constant Comment with a friend. Maybe some
zucchini bread.

Meet with honors students from 1 to 4. At the community
college I tried to incite them to poetry. Convince them this line
of work, beat the bejesus out of a gig as gizzard splitter at the
processing plant or cleaning up after a leak at the germ warfare
center. Be all you can be, wrap a rubber band around your
trigger finger until it drops off.

Swim at 10 before picking up B, before demo on the
green, and before meeting Moss, if it isn't too crowded. Only
three old women talking about their daughters-in-law last
Wednesday at 10.

Phone hardware to see if radon test arrived.

Keep an eye out for a new yellow blanket. Left B's on the
plane, though he seems over it already. Left most recent issue of
Z in the seat. That will make a few businessmen boil. I liked the
man who sat next to me, he was sweet to B. Hated flying, said
he never let all of his weight down.

Need to get books in the mail today. Make time pass in line at
the P.O. imagining man in front of me butt naked. Fellow in the
good-preacher-blue suit, probably has a cold, hard bottom.

Call N for green tomato recipe. Have to get used to the
Yankee growing season. If this is Wednesday, N goes in hospital
today. Find out how long after marrow transplant before can visit.

Mother said she read in paper that Pete was granted a divorce.
His third. My highschool boyfriend. Meanest thing I could have
done, I did to him, returning a long-saved-for engagement
ring in a Band-Aid box, while he was stationed in Da Nang.

Meant to tell F this morning about dream of eating grasshoppers, fried but happy. Our love a difficult instrument we are learning to play. Practice, practice.

No matter where I call home anymore, feel like a boat under the trees. Living is strange.

This week only; bargain on laid paper at East Side Copy Shop.

Woman picking her nose at the stoplight. Shouldn't look, only privacy we have anymore in the car. Isn't that the woman from the colloquium last fall, who told me she was a stand-up environmentalist. What a wonderful trade, I said, because the evidence of planetary wrongdoing is overwhelming. Because because because of the horrible things we do.

If this is Wednesday, meet F at Health Department at 10:45 for AIDS test.

If this is Wednesday, it's trash night.

Just Whistle: a valentine

KELSEY STREET PRESS, 1993

A Brief and Blameless Outline of the Ontogeny of Crow

Tonight one said   Bluets the other said

Goosefoot one said   Hungry the other said

Hangnail it said   Spanish bayonet it said

Daylilies it said   Hotel it said

Matches it said   Sickle senna it said

Feverfew the one said   Headache the other said

Panties it said   Panic grass it said

Clotbur it said   Backdoor it would say

Tickets the one said   Purslane it would say

Morning glories said one   Money said the other

Whistle it said   Asshole it thought it said

BECAUSE CONDITIONS ARE IDEAL FOR CROWING the singers
flock to this spot. They rageth they seizeth they penetrateth
and maketh us to lie down by the roaring waters. By day they
take the longstem roses to our backdoor. They secure us to
trellises. They whip us breathless. This includes the pool
painter whose hands are perpetually blue. Aquatic. Transbluent.
One hand signs the blued canvas of our body. Other hands.
Cigaretted. Hired hands. Dripping paint on the plush carpet.
They set a different set of teeth to each teat. Spit like
grasshoppers. In the eden of their woods, dogs glom. Warm
winds stir them up. They let the flightless birds peck our feet.
We hold mirrors. Bloody our lip under the rent in the
backdoor. They crow us for the quick and the dead and on
the third day they rise and crow us again. Very soon now we can
return to our life of wonder and regret.

On the Eve of Their Mutually Assured Destruction:

The body would open its legs like a book
letting the soft pencils of light
fall on its pages, like doors
into a hothouse, belladonna blooming there:
it would open like a wine list, a mussel, wings

To be mounted without tearing:
it would part its legs in the forest
and let the fronds impress themselves in the resin
of its limbs, smoothen the rump
of the other body like a horse's. To wit:

The whole world would not be lost.

Let the record show the body
has made identical claims before
though never in the wake of its flensing.

Voice of the Ridge

Something about a hazy afternoon—a long drive
    about cedars spearing the sky
Something about a body at a crossing
    about a dog missing a paw
    about buying a freshly dressed hen
Something about the locus of the dead

Something about a strange town on a weekend
    about large white panties on a line
About a table in a family-owned cafe
    an old morsel on the tines
Something about the owner dragging one foot
Something about wine from a jelly glass

Something about a hazy afternoon—a long drive
    about no purse no stockings
Something about unfolding the map
    about a cemetery that isn't kept up
    about grasshoppers—their knack for surprise
Something about finding a full set of clothes in the weeds

Something about a hazy afternoon—a long drive
    about hills of goldenrod
Something about filling-station attendants
    the one blue hole in the clouds
Something about birds of prey—the locus of the dead

Something about the long drive home—a slow sundowning
    about the din of insects
Something about straight gold hair on a pillow
Something about writing by the kingly light
    in the quick minutes left before lips
    suction a nipple from wrinkled linen

Tremble

ECCO PRESS, 1996

Approximately Forever

She was changing on the inside
it was true what had been written

The new syntax of love
both sucked and burned

The secret clung around them
She took in the smell

Walking down a road to nowhere
every sound was relevant

The sun fell behind them now
he seemed strangely moved

She would take her clothes off
for the camera

she said in plain english
but she wasn't holding that snake

Because Fulfillment Awaits

An arm reaching back through a hole in a ceiling
for a box of poison   "Now"   the dark talks
"I hate being a man"   An arm offering a box of poison
in the direction   of a hole in the ceiling
A handkerchief offered   "Wait"
comes the warning from below   "Cover yourself"

Even in touching   retouching
steeped in words   in the proliferation and cancellation
of words   one tends to forget   one forgets
the face   the human face   One wants
to create a bright   new past   one creates it

Oneness

As surely as it is about air
    about light and about earth

Water will seep between fingers
    gathered in a gentle fist

For what good a wooden fence
    against breath fuming with fire

What good to point out the flower path
    if the sugar bag is empty

What good blowing the clarinet
    if blowing only makes one ugly

For as surely as wind unlocks
    car doors and cabinets

Young men wander off with their testes
    to part the perineum's grasses

And when they come to the little stream
    each tenses against the other

And against anything unforeseen
    and under each pair of skin

She discovers his unassailable otherness
    and under each pair of skin

He discovers her moisture, dark, fecundity
    for as surely as it is about air

About light and about earth
    gathered in a gentle fist

Water will seep between fingers
    for the unknown must remain unknown

I know that and you know that
    flesh of my flesh, bone of my bone

What Keeps

We live on a hillside
close to water
We eat in darkness
We sleep in the coldest
part of the house
We love in silence
We keep our poetry
locked in a glass cabinet
Some nights We stay up
passing it back and
forth
between us
drinking deep

Key Episodes from an Earthly Life

As surely as there are crumbs on the lips
of the blind   I came for a reason

I remember when the fields were no taller
than a pencil   do you remember that

I told him   I've got socks older than her
but he would not listen

You will starve out girl   they told her
but she did not listen

As surely as there is rice in the cuffs
of the priest   sex is a factor   not a fact

Everything I do is leaning   toward
what we came for   is that perfectly clear

I like your shoes your uncut hair
I like your use of space too

I wanted to knock her lights out
the air cut in and did us some good

One thing about my television set it has
a knob on it enabling me to switch channels

Now it is your turn   to shake or
provoke   or heal me   I won't say it again

Do you like your beets well-cooked and chilled
even if they make your gums itch

Those dark arkansas roads   that is the sound
I am after   the choiring of crickets

Around this time of year   especially evening
I love everything   I sold enough eggs

To buy a new dress   I watched him drink the juice
of our beets   And render the light liquid

I came to talk you into physical splendor
I do not wish to speak to your machine

In a Piercing and Sucking Species

he doesn't see anybody
in the tree
nor does she see anybody

in the grass he wires
that wiring her
he gets erect

reading this very wire
in the grass
she gets wet

the presence of his absence
disturbs the absence
of his presence sometimes

more sometimes less
in dreams they go forward
without hunger without faces

others fall off the limb
but she does not fall
she pierces him

everywhere and nobody else
when she returns
she seizes him

in quivering mandibles
relieved
to find him

unchewed
newly in leaf

Crescent

In recent months I have become intent on seizing happiness: to this end I applied various shades of blue: only the evening is outside us now propagating honeysuckle: I am trying to invent a new way of moving under my dress: the room squares off against this: watch the water glitter with excitement: when we cut below the silver skin of the surface the center retains its fluidity: do I still remind you of a locust clinging to a branch: I give you an idea of the damages: you would let edges be edges: believe me: when their eyes poured over your long body of poetry I also was there: when they laid their hands on your glass shade I also was there: when they put their whole trust in your grace I had to step outside to get away from my cravenness: we have done these things to each other without benefit of a mirror: unlike the honeysuckle goodness does not overtake us: yet the thigh keeps quiet under nylon: later beneath the blueness of trees the future falls out of place: something always happens: draw nearer my dear: never fear: the world spins nightly toward its brightness and we are on it

Everything Good Between Men and Women

has been written in mud and butter
and barbecue sauce. The walls and
the floors used to be gorgeous.
The socks off-white and a near match.
The quince with fire blight
but we get two pints of jelly
in the end. Long walks strengthen
the back. You with a fever blister
and myself with a sty. Eyes
have we and we are forever prey
to each other's teeth. The torrents
go over us. Thunder has not harmed
anyone we know. The river coursing
through us is dirty and deep. The left
hand protects the rhythm. Watch
your head. No fires should be
unattended. Especially when wind. Each
receives a free Swiss Army knife.
The first few tongues are clearly
preparatory. The impression
made by yours I carry to my grave. It is
just so sad so creepy so beautiful.
Bless it. We have so little time
to learn, so much . . . The river
courses dirty and deep. Cover the lettuce.
Call it a night. O soul. Flow on. Instead.

Morning Star

This isn't the end. It simply
cannot be the end. It is a road.
You go ahead coatless, light-
soaked, more rutilant than
the road. The soles of your shoes
sparkle. You walk softly
as you move further inside
your subject. It is a living
season. The trees are anxious
to be included. The car with fins
beams through countless
oncoming points of rage and need.
The sloughed-off cells
under our bed form little hills
of dead matter. If the most sidereal
drink is pain, the most soothing
clock is music. A poetry
of shine could come of this.
It will be predominantly
green. You will be allowed
to color in as much as you want
for green is good
for the teeth and the eyes.

Flame

the breath   the trees   the bridge

the road   the rain   the sheen

the breath   the line   the skin

the vineyard   the fences   the leg

the water   the breath   the shift

the hair   the wheels   the shoulder

the breath   the lane   the streak

the lining   the hour   the reasons

the name   the distance   the breath

the scent   the dogs   the blear

the lungs   the breath   the glove

the signal   the turn   the need

the steps   the lights   the door

the mouth   the tongue   the eyes

the burn   the burned   the burning

Deepstep Come Shining

COPPER CANYON PRESS, 1998

It's the year of the magicicadae. Seventeen years underground. Boring slowly upward. Ever so slowly. To get to the surface in the spring of the seventeenth year, it will scrabble through pavement. With not a minute to spare except for sex and song.

It must escape its carapace. Quickly. We must all escape our carapace. Come shining.

The day animals need to be able to distinguish colors. And the night creatures must manage low levels of light.

The white piano *is* her mother. And it fills with petals. Ghost hair. Who shot the piano. Killed the mother. And made the daughter to suffer.

The cat has guanine in the retina. Extra sensitive. In Yeats's version Oscar Wilde's father enucleates his patient's eye at the dining-room table and the cat eats it. "Cats love eyes," the cat lover reassures his patient.

Onionlight. Vidalia onions. That's right. Now do you know where you are.

The boneman said apply flax and whites of eggs to bleeding eyes.

So Gloucester had to smell his way to Dover.

But we aren't going there. Or anywhere the air does not smell of barbecue.

The preacher considers Whitey's Drive-In his parish.

What did you buy at the 20-cent table.

Where do you folks live at. Between the *a* and the *t*.

Take a mirror to the river. Then what. The young woman shuffles into the boneman's shed, and he brings her a jar of fermented swamp mulch from the closet. To make the swelling go down. Leglight.

*

There are enough signs. Of the lack of tenderness in the world. And yet. And yet. All you have to do is ask. Anyone here can extol the virtues of an onion. Where to get barbecue minced, pulled, or chopped. The hour of the day they have known the thorn of love.

*

Stop at Bulldog's will you for a six-pack of Icehouse.

The cornea does the work. The back wall is the retina.

Just a drop of silver nitrate in the newborn's eyes. It's the law. In case of syphilis. Thus are we treated as thieves in a department store and syphilitics in a hospital. Even the newborn gets *the treatment.*

We live by the etcetera principle.

All the cool people liked the children's humping line dance. All the rest were horrified.

When in Rome . . .

By the rays of Light I understand its least parts, how my life does not appear in cursive, but in handwrit letters. Crudely executed.

SALVATION. DON'T LEAVE EARTH WITHOUT IT.

Ma'am, are these your glasses.

Here we live and breathe in all the glory of this Vidalia onion. Lengths of pecan trees whipping by. Coming soon. In all his glory. Suddenly I have the feeling of a great victory. A delirious brilliance. Onionlight.

Corner of Hamlet and Bridges. A Jazz Messiah was born here 9/23/26. That's one little step for a man. Seven or eight Giant

Steps for mankind. Empty, plate-glass light of Hamlet, North Carolina.

The door locked and the blue room opens only for private parties.

Don't touch that dial.

In the town with the clothesline ordinance the women are bleaching their teeth.

She has Casa Blanca lilies. I covet.

The fiddle contest will take place rain or shine.

*

The Colonel's curtains whiten in unelaborating rays. His clawfoot tubs. Big-tub love.

What's that spot on the wall. That light saucer.

She wanted to fall to her knees under petals of snow. In a stark white dormitory. Twelve white cakes would be brought to a cloth-draped table by twelve starched women. All of this mystery, mystery, mystery.

If I can't coax a twelve-foot tomato plant to yield one juicy mouthful. I must be under a curse.

What if we stay here long enough to attend a stranger's funeral. I like this spot.

And when the sudarium was removed, wrap by wrap . . .
Too late the doctor said. You will never see.

Look-alikes fall in love. Unless . . .

O my irises. My irises. O the sidewalls of my breasts.

It reminds me of my back life. If I had stayed I would have married the no-count. He couldn't help it. He had no luck. They took his luck and tied it to a rabbit's neck.

Trailer living was appealing when I was seventeen.

We need a preponderance of love.

Ride. Eat. Sleep. It said on his T-shirt.

The darkness will eat you. They say in Bosnia.

The LED emits the following diode: This is the time to see and to feel WHOLES.

Color. Degree of brightness. Saturation: Hue. Value. Chroma. He had a passion for nomenclature.

Ride. Eat. Sleep

Oncet   after a heavy rain

he come back   at daybreak

threw down a few dollars and cents

alongside a set   of pretty glass eyes

into a little dish on the dresser

flopped crosswise on the bed and slept

I started to write   I feel lost here

and I'm going to go home   Oncet

I clave to him   like fog but the bus

at Dahlonega   wasn't waiting for me

to go through the old lucubrations

and Brother Veal of Deepstep nor was I

Could I have a touch of your vitreous humor.

What does she look like, the handsome young blind man asked
his pretty, freckled girl at the festival.

She has black hair. Strange, he said. I pictured her blond.

The rain would let up and then it would start up. Some brought
umbrellas. Some turned garbage bags into ponchos.

The refrain to the rain would be a movement up and down the
clefs of light.

The boats in the bay took in the festival from the water.

Blur in. Blur out.

The darkness will eat you.

A bullet don't have nobody's name on it.

HAIR TODAY. GONE TOMORROW. (sign at the electrolysis center)
Dontouchmymustache. That's all the Japanese I can say.

They didn't have a metal detector. So you know folks were
packing. Club Paradise. Saturday night. Bowlegs Miller led the
house band.

> What are you going to do when our lamps are gone out.
> What are you going to do.
> What are you going to do when you come to the crossroad.

Everybody in this clinic needs love. A preponderance of love.

The eye is an image-catching device. On this much we are agreed.

They dropped silver nitrate in my new baby's eyes. According to law. A poisonous colorless crystalline compound. Used in manufacturing photographic film, silvering mirrors, dyeing hair, plating silver, and in medicine as a cautery and antiseptic.

```
ST P H       F P L T
ST P H       F P L T
   T P    EUR    S
                 T
      HR  EU     T
S         EU PB G S
T      O
S   H A          D
       O         S
            F P L T
T
S   H A          D
       O         S
   PW          B G
T P HRAO         D
                 D
   W
   PW R O        D
   W  A     R B
                 S
            F
TK    A     R B G
            F P L T
   W  A     R B
            F P L T
      A          S
                 T
TK    A     R B G
   K    O     P L S
        E  PB
T         EUR
   HR  EU
T P H
T      O         TS
       O     PB
            F P L T
   W  A     R B
            F P L T
T
   HR  EU        T
             B G
        E        T
        E  PB
            F P L T
TK       E
S     R O U R    D
            F P L T
S     A
T P H O      R
             U   S
S           E R  T
            EU
            F    T
TK    A     R B G
            F P L T
   W  A     E
S         E     TS
                 T
      H A    PB G
```

*

After he lost his sight, he could discriminate colors by their vibration. He was thrown to the ground under the power.

The water here, black marble. The grass, army-surplus green.

Poking around in the woods with a gun. Poke around in the house with a book. Poke around. Poke around.

They bleach their teeth those women.

Are those Casa Blanca lilies. I covet.

We lunch on Onion River. Stop by Cloud's Fly Shop.

Fiddle contest tomorrow rain or shine.

Get the hell out of here, can't you see I'm not dressed. Can't you see I'm depressed.

I see. I see.

Please don't put your feet on the chairs, it said in the eye doctor's office. Please don't spit on the floor, it said in my father's courtroom.

Her Aunt Flo said she hadn't had any in so long she'd done growed back together.

Are you still working on that drink.

Cold pop. Free air. Sold here.

We never close. Every nickel counts. Just ask Big Sam. He suctioned every nickel from every small town pocket and he sewed it under his lids, a veritable sheik from Arkansas.

He put a pillow over her mother's head and shot her. The white piano shivered in the corner like a boy with an orchid.

That was a helluva note.

After the iridectomy
she fell to the ground under the power

The boxwoods that lined the road
were walking with her

She could touch the willow wands on the other side of Little
Lynches River

She smudged the passage she had once felt

She was fearful of putting a morsel of cake
in her mouth

She thought it too large to enter in

A pool of shade appeared bottomless

The contours of a man were horrible to her
those of the family dog were bearable

A pool of shade appeared bottomless

Two white horses side by side. Going to take her on her farewell ride.

Ain't it hawd.

Half-fare, blind, mmhmm.

Nothing in the world beats time.

She said her sister was more like Aunt Flo everyday. Big blond Aunt Flora with the smutty mouth who said she hadn't had any in so long it'd done growed back together.

In the gated communities the women are bleaching their teeth.

Shielding her eyes among her Casa Blanca lilies with a tad of a hangover she offers spiderweb to staunch his paper cut.

Cloud's Fly Shop in spitting distance.

Fiddle contest rain or shine, declares the flyer on the creosote pole.

I see. I see.

Don't you just hate it when your gown catches between your buttocks.

Don't you just hate it when the waiter says, Are you still working on that drink.

Poke around. Poke around. Can't you see I'm depressed. Welcome to my sensorium. You can touch, but you cannot lie.

You must know the Veals of Deepstep.

Mother's neighbor passes on her mower, riding (*sic*) her Clancy novel.

She suffers from what Wittgenstein called aspect blindness. Is it a rabbit. Nay, it's a swan, a swan.

Cooling Time: An American Poetry Vigil

COPPER CANYON PRESS, 2005

from **Op-Ed**

Every year the poem I most want to write, the poem that would in effect allow me to stop writing, changes shapes, changes directions. It refuses to come forward, to stand still while I move to meet it, embrace and coax it to sit on the porch with me and watch the lightning bugs steal behind the fog's heavy veil, listen for the drag of johnboats through the orchestra of locusts and frogs. An old handplow supports the mailbox, a split-rail fence borders the front lot. Hollyhocks and sunflowers loom there. At the end of the lot the road forks off to the left toward the river, to the right toward the old chicken slaughterhouse. The poem hangs back, wraithlike, yet impenetrable as briar. The porch is more impressive than the rest of the house. A moth as big as a girl's hand spreads itself out on the screendoor. The house smells like beets. For in this poem it is always Arkansas, summer, evening. But in truth, the poem never sleeps unless I do, for if I were to come upon it sleeping, I would net it. And that would be that, my splendid catch.

*

We must do something with our time on this small aleatory sphere for motives other than money. Power is not an acceptable surrogate.[†]

I am even willing to argue passion is what separates us from other life-forms—that is, beyond the power to reason is our ability to escape from the desert of pure reason by its own primary instrument, language. And if it be poetry that makes

---

† The eclectic Bulgarian scholar Elias Canetti fastidiously stylized his 550-page study *Crowds and Power* to conclude simply, "To be the last man to remain alive is the deepest urge of every real seeker after power."

the words flesh, then it is no less or more escapable than our bodies. But it is at least that free.

Veering in the elusory direction of freedom, I would submit, it is a function of poetry to locate those zones inside us that would be free and declare them so. Always there are restrictions: as traditional conventions are more or less disavowed, others remain constant for longer periods, and another is revived after long periods of disuse. Poetry without form is a fiction. But that there is a freedom in words is the larger fact, and in poetry, where formal restrictions can bear down heavily, it is important to remember the cage is never locked.

I have been a keen but unsystematic student of book-length poems, in substance and design. Length admits them to the novel's province of inclusivity and digression, but redoubles the requisite for form. The need for form arises not so much for containment but for support. Form naturally determines the poem's movement, whether it be gradual, teleological, furious, or traveling in reverse. Otherwise, the stasis of art prose. Ugh.

from **Concerning Complexity**

I like to come and go through different doors more than I like
to throw my weight against the same one every time only to
discover it was hollow as Hollywood or never even locked,

and I like to change the locks once in a while, too; but it isn't
just about keeping it interesting for Author, Author or Dear
Reader;

it is about how differently things actually play out if you come
and go by different portals, long live la différence; as for tran-
scendence, well baby, that is the sun's job.

from **Just Looking:**

Begin with nothing, remote starting point, the area of darkest color. Begin with nothing, which is yourself, Eternal Stranger, the poem that always acts alone. The poem supplies its references from its own surround. Sounds its own memory. The mind of the poem passes along interior surfaces. One does not contact the poem's ground without feeling bound to its secrecy. Its spans reach in both directions; they appear as tangible lengths across an opening. They attach to neither side. They duplicate themselves. And you, who are nothing, are duplicated on them. Moving. Dizzy with motion and altitude, but unafraid. See, it is just as you imagined it would be. And everything we have known, which is nothing, lines up, as do our friends, who are immanent in the lustrous element of the bridges themselves. And we who are nothing, along with everything we have known, which is nothing, have learned to listen so deeply, we have learned to say it with *silence our native tongue;* with a fluency that distributes both sound and light just so, until there is no horror vacui left in us. The unfathomable emptiness, negation, loss, absence have themselves become filling if not fulfilling. The poem is not given to nattering punctuation; the coextensive conjunction. W.S. Merwin's "The Bridges" never fails to remind me of Glenn Gould's pronouncement: "The purpose of art is not the release of a momentary ejection of adrenaline, but a gradual lifelong construction of a state of wonder and serenity."

from **Collaborating**

I was born in a warren of no great distinction in the vicinity of the middle hillbilly class. There, with progressive effort (gravity never sleeps), I will possibly grow quite old (the women do in my family), and indisputably shall I die. I am the daughter of an annually retired judge who has lived and worked inside the tawny leather bindings of jurisprudence for well over half a century. For this man words themselves have become palpable, material, and even law. And I am the daughter of a woman whose manipulations of the stenotype machine, crossword puzzle, and telephone have likewise been exhaustively verbal. Both of them are autochthons of the rural Arkansas Ozarks. The paternal side issues from a farming community named Cisco that no longer salaries a postal clerk to raise our country's flag (nor has it since the flag wore forty-nine stars). The distaff side hails from the bluffs of a beautiful swift river in a moribund railroad town whose rock buildings have been mortared back into service by a German manufacturer of work uniforms.

It is poetry that remarks on the barely perceptible disappearances from our world such as that of the sleeping porch or the root cellar. And poetry that notes the barely perceptible appearances.

It falls on the sweet neck of poetry to keep the rain-pitted face of love from leaving us once and for all.

*

Poets should exceed themselves—when demands on us are slack, we should be anything but. Pressing the demands of the word forward is not only relevant but urgent. If our country does not vigorously cultivate poetry, it is either poetry's ineluctable time to wither or time to make a promise on its own behalf to put out new shoots and insist on a much bigger pot.

Give physical, material life to the words. Record what you see. Rise, walk, and make a day. Grandmother Wright oft bade the latter.

from **Five of Us Drove to Horatio:**

Every word I set down rightly involves overcoming an
ingrained resistance to do otherwise.

The Ozarks are a fixture in my mindscape, but I did not stay
local in every respect. I always think of Miles Davis, "People
who don't change end up like folk musicians playing in muse-
ums, local as a motherfucker." I would not describe my attach-
ment to home as ghostly, but long-distanced. My ear has been
licked by so many other tongues.

The lacunae are there even if you are working against a wall of
sound. There are gaps in everything. What is lineation if it is
not about respecting the surrounding space. And the spaces
in between.

It is fair to say I am interested in the formally anomalous poem,
not the representatively formal poet, that is, when it comes
to discrete poems. When it comes to extended poems, I am
interested in a structure that is supportable, bottom up, as
well as structure within the larger one, which will activate
the whole.

Poetry and Parenting

are symbiotic—the relationship is close, protracted and not necessarily of benefit one to the other. They are different organisms, different species. There are certainly periods when they fill each other up, and there are just as certainly periods when they drain each other's cup. It is not my choice to forgo one for the other. I was asked by a poet, who had reluctantly chosen not to have children, what conditions I would require to become the best poet I could. And I had to allow, I had them, though I struggle for the opportunities to enter that clearing where I am alone and afraid and humbled and pregnant only with the anticipation of working without interruption. I had to allow that I require the distraction, that I require the attachment, and that unencumbered I merely dissipate; I come undone. I had to admit, I require the struggle though it brings me to my knees when I most long to be standing free.

This Much I Know:

Poetry will not go quietly. You would have to starve it out, and it can eat on very little. Hunger and love move the world, didn't Schiller say so.

in our only time.

"Follow me," the voice, the long, longed-for voice stops

the writing hand. "I have your shoes." Except

for a rotating fan, movement at a minimum. The plan,

if one can call it a plan, is to be in what is known

to some as the perennial present; beginning

with a few sentences written in a kitchen while others

cling to their own images in twisted sheets of heat.

A napkin floats from a counter in lieu of a letter. Portals

of the back life part in silence: O verge

of song, O big eyelets of daylight. Leaving milk and bowl

on the table, leaving the house discalced. All this

mystery, mildly erotic. Even if one is terrified

of both death and the color red. Even if a message is sent

each of us in secrecy, no one can make it stay.

Notwithstanding scale—everything has its meaning,

every thing matters; no one a means every one an end

One Big Self: An Investigation

TWIN PALMS PRESS, 2003; COPPER CANYON PRESS, 2007

Stripe for Stripe

Driving through this part of Louisiana you can pass four prisons in less than an hour. "The spirit of every age," writes Eric Schlosser, "is manifest in its public works." So this is who we are, the jailers, the jailed. This is the spirit of our age.

"You won't be back, will you?" asked the inmate who told me he wanted to be a success.

Try to remember it the way it was. Try to remember what I wore when I visited the prisons. Trying to remember how tall was my boy then. What books was I teaching. Trying to remember how I hoped to add one true and lonely word to the host of texts that bear upon incarceration.

Something about the extra-realism of that peculiar institution caused me to balk, also the resistance of poetry to the conventions of evidentiary writing, notwithstanding top-notch examples to the contrary: Mandelstam, Akhmatova, Wilde, Valéry, Celan, Desnos, et al. After all, I am not them. She asked me to come down, my friend the photographer, and I went, and then I wanted to see if my art could handle that hoe.

Trying to remember how my skin felt when I opened an envelope of proofs of Deborah Luster's intimate aluminum portraits of the inmates at Transylvania (the site of East Carroll Parish Prison Farm, a minimum-security male prison, now closed); then Angola (the site of Louisiana State Penitentiary, maximum security); then St. Gabriel (the site of the Louisiana Correctional Institution for Women, the LCIW). I was electrified by the first face—a young, handsome man blowing smoke out of his nose. Behind every anonymous number, a very specific face.

On the phone my friend described to me the rich Delta grounds of Angola, 18,000 acres. Angola, where the topsoil is measured not in inches but feet. The former sugarcane plantation lies at the confluence of rivers and borderland of the unruly Tunica Hills. Grey pelicans nest on the two prison lakes, alongside the airstrip, the grading sheds, the endless fields of okra and corn. Then there's the prison museum, the prison radio station, the prison magazine; the tracking horses and tracking dogs trained by inmates . . . and the tree-lined neighborhood of free-world residents, their children bused outside the fence to school. Then the immaculate cinder-block buildings that house the inmates, the administration building, and the death house; the greenhouse and extensive flower beds— take away the fencing and it resembles nothing so much as a college campus. The men in maximum number more than the men who lived in my hometown. Then there's the geriatric unit, the award-winning hospice program; the caisson the inmates built to bear the men in the hand-built coffins to one of the two graveyards inside the prison. In the old burial ground most graves are not identified by name. The caisson is pulled by draft horses, French Quarter style. When the champion of the prison rodeo had a heart attack in the fields, a riderless horse led the final procession. The celebrated inmate's uniform was "retired" to the prison museum.

Everything about Louisiana seems to constitute itself differently from everywhere else in the Union: the food, the idiom, the stuff in the trees, the critters in the water, and the laws, Napoleonic, not mother-country common law. The prisons inevitably mirror differences found in the free world. Where they came up with their mirrors is another mystery. (In maximum, they are made of metal.) The definition of the face is a memory.

Vivid to me is Debbie saying that at the trial of her mother's murderer, she looked around and saw the people sitting on separate sides of the courtroom, the way they do at a wedding, the bride's people, the groom's people, and she tried to take in the damage radiating through the distinct lines—the perpetrator's side, the victim's side.

Vivid to me is leaving Angola after the first visit and Debbie asking what I thought, and I said (too fast) I thought those were the nicest people I had ever met, and the ironic laughter it provoked in us both, the car yawing. The obvious truth, people are people. Equally, the damage is never limited to perpetrator and victim. Also, that the crimes are not the sum of the criminal any more than anyone is entirely separable from their acts.

I remember an afternoon at the iron pile at Transylvania watching the men plait each other's hair between sets at the weight bench. When I asked about a man whose face was severely scarred, a very specific face, with large, direct aquamarine eyes, a guard told me that the man's brother had thrown a tire over his head and set it on fire. This I did not know how to absorb. It was a steaming day; the men were lifting weights and plaiting their hair.

I remember Easter weekend at the women's prison. The day before, a long line formed outside the prison-run beauty shop. Inside, the women having their hair fixed were talking back to the soap operas on the small snowy screen. By visiting day the inner courtyard had been transformed into a theme park for the children. A trampoline had been rented, a cotton-candy machine; someone dressed in a bunny suit was organizing an egg hunt. The little girls wore starched, flouncy dresses, and the boys white jackets and black, clip-on bow ties. The women were dressed up, too, even the ones shackled at the ankle and waist. Deborah photographed all day, nonstop. Identifiable pictures of children would have to be excluded from publication, but people wanted a keepsake. We left before visiting hours ended. It wasn't our place to be there. It wasn't really in us to be there.

Remember sitting in the frigid Holiday Inn bar near St. Gabriel, at the end of one visit to the women's prison, staring at the aquarium, not talking.

I talked to a man who told me he has done a lot of time. Lot of time. He should write a book, he said. He wants to be a success. "Hollywood, huh, here I come."

I talked to a woman who said the one time her dad visited her from the Midwest, she asked him to look at her eyes. There was a look she didn't want to get, a faraway look. Her father pretended to examine her eyes, then told her they looked like the same old peepers to him. She passed her time reading. Same way she passed her childhood. She thought she was going to be an astronomer when she grew up. Not a felon.

Both parents are dead now. Of her three sons, one disappeared, one died of suicide, and the third severed contact.

One of the inmates at St. Gabriel informed me she wouldn't be around for visiting hours tomorrow because she was on the drill team. Also, her ex-husband would not be bringing her little boy to see her. Not tomorrow, not ever.

The grease burns, I am told by another inmate, are courtesy of her sister.

DON'T WALK ON THE GRASS, says the sign posted in the inner yard.

The coffin builder (now deceased) in the prison was so devoted to his catahoula he overfed her to the point that she could only walk side to side. She wore a red halter he fashioned for her. Sissy was the dog's name. His name was Redwine.

The inmate who fishes one of the stocked lakes for the warden admitted that his son was in prison, too, in another state. He saw him once when he was a baby. And then, once, between sentences.

A guard pointed out a woman whose father, mother, uncle, brother, sister were all locked up, two were at Hunt, two here, and one at Big Gola. Her sister was her fall partner. It made you wonder who was left to look after the dog.

That day Debbie was photographing mothers and daughters, and twins.

Another guard told me he had made the mistake he had most dreaded making, delivering the execution letter, setting the date and the time, to the wrong man on death row.

In some prisons, you can't have a last cigarette, but Valium is permitted.

I heard about a petition in a town out West to take back the night sky. The locals thought they were getting a second minimum-security prison, an economic pick-me-up. Instead, a supermax sprang up, that perverse marriage of mind and technology. Lights from the new institution burn so intensely the stars have gone dark on them.

Then there's the bus that leaves from Monroe taking visitors to one of four neighboring pens, Al Derry's Prison Transport and Popcorn Balls. Evidently, the popcorn balls make it the competitive ride. Only in Louisiana.

After a time. A lot of time. They stop coming. The free-worlders. They are too poor or too busy working or are already looking after others on the outside or their car is broken or they are too worn down or they move too far off or they get old, sick, and die. So the inmates wait for their turn.

They aren't going anywhere. They have all the time there is.

"The only continuity of our lives," wrote Malcolm Braly, American writer, American lifer, "was that we had none."

"Waiting," goes the motto at St. Gabriel, "it's the LCIW way."

I wrote a woman and asked if she ever had any pets. She wrote back: Bandit, Baby, Snobby, Elsie, Bear (those were the dogs). Tiger and Fuzzball (the cats), Jill, Ben, and Junior (the coons). "And a lot of un-named fish, hamsters, rabbits, chickens, ducks, geese, guinea pigs, and a deer, not really a pet but I finally coaxed to the point she would eat out of my hand."

Not to idealize, not to judge, not to exonerate, not to aestheticize immeasurable levels of pain. Not to demonize, not anathematize. What I wanted was to unequivocally lay out the real feel of hard time. I wanted it given to understand that when you pass four prisons in less than an hour, the countryside's apparent emptiness is more legible. It is an open, running comment when the only spike in employment statistics is being created by the supply of people crossing the line.

I wanted the banter, the idiom, the soft-spoken cadence of Louisiana speech to cut through the mass-media myopia. I wanted the heat, the humidity, the fecundity of Louisiana to travel right up the body. What I wanted was to convey the sense of normalcy for which humans strive under conditions that are anything but what we in the free world call normal, no matter what we may have done for which we were never charged.

The world of the prison system springs up adjacent to the free world. As the towns decline, the prisons grow. As industries disappear, prisons proliferate; state-funded prison-building surges are complemented by private investment promising "to be an integral component of your corrections strategy," according to an industry founder. The interrelation of poverty, illiteracy, substance and physical abuse, mental illness, race, and gender to the prison population is blaring to the naked eye and borne out in the statistics. Of the developed nations, only Russia approaches our rate of incarceration. And the Big Bear is a distant second. Ladies and Gentlemen of the Jury, the warp in the mirror is of our making.

The popular perception is that art is apart. I insist it is a part of. Something not in dispute is that people in prison are apart from. If you can accept—whatever level of discipline and punishment you adhere to momentarily aside—that the ultimate goal should be to reunite the separated with the larger human enterprise, it might behoove us to see prisoners, among others, as they elect to be seen, in their larger selves. If we go there, if not with our bodies then at least our minds, we are more likely to register the implications.

✠ ✠ ✠

I am going to prison.

I am going to visit three prisons in Louisiana.

I am going on the heels of my longtime friend Deborah Luster, a photographer.

It is a summons.

All roads are turning into prison roads.

I already feel guilty.

I haven't done anything.

But I allow the mental pull in both directions.

I am going to prison in order to write about it. Like a nineteenth-century traveler.

Kafka put it this way, "Guilt is never to be doubted."

Also: behind every anonymous number, a very specific face.

Also: there are more than two million individuals, in this country, whose sentences have rendered them more or less invisible. Many of them permanently.

First to Transylvania. Then Angola. Then St. Gabriel. These are their place-names.

Over the next year and a half Deborah Luster will photograph upwards of 1,500 inmates.

I will make three trips.

It is an almost imperceptible gesture, a flick of the conscience, to go, to see, but I will be wakeful.

It is a summons.

*

Count your fingers

Count your toes

Count your nose holes

Count your blessings

Count your stars (lucky or not)

Count your loose change

Count the cars at the crossing

Count the miles to the state line

Count the ticks you pulled off the dog

Count your calluses

Count your shells

Count the points on the antlers

Count the newjack's keys

Count your cards; cut them again

*

If I were you:

Screw up today, and it's solitary, Sister Woman, the padded dress with the
food log to gnaw upon. This is where you enter the eye of the fart. The air
is foul. The dirt is gumbo. Avoid all physical contact. Come nightfall the
bugs will carry you off.

 I don't have a clue, do I.

If you were me:

If you wanted blueberries you could have a big bowl. Two dozen bushes
right on your hill. And thornless raspberries at the bottom. Walk bare-
footed; there's no glass. If you want to kiss your kid you can. If you want a
Porsche, buy it on the installment plan. You have so many good books
you can't begin to count them. Walk the dog to the bay every living day.
The air is salted. Septembers you can hear the blues jumping before
seeing water through the vault in the leaves. Watch the wren nesting in
the sculpture by the shed. Smoke if you feel like it. Or swim. Call a friend.
Or keep perfectly still. The mornings are free.

If I were a felon I'd be home now.

Bienvenu en Louisiane

The septuagenarian murderer knits nonstop

One way to wear out the clock

In Tickfaw miracles occur

This weekend: the thirteenth annual Cajun joke contest

They will / will not be sending the former governor to Big Gola

I pinch a cigarette and stare at Rachel's wrist scars

By their color they are recent

That the eye not be drawn in

I suggest all courage is artificial

Her sister did not fail

Noses amuse us and hers not less so

> short   smart   butch
> utterly unsure of herself

Whichever you see as sadder

A jukebox or a coffin

A woman's hand will close your eyes

On the surface she is receptive

I wear the lenses of my time

Some run to type, but I am not qualified

Hectored by questions that have to do with the Forms of Harm,
    the Nature of the Beast, Mercy, etc.

Last seen yesterday morning in a one-piece swimsuit

The popular 16-year-old is 5′ 7″, 127 lbs

The K-9 unit given her long white prom gloves, her pillowcase

Do you wish to save these changes
    yes   no   never mind

The stinging caterpillars of Tickfaw pour onto the bark
    in the form of a cross

A random book skimmed from the women's shelf

In which an undine-like maiden
    is espyed feeding white daisies to a bear

Something on anarcho-syndicalism wasn't really expected

    poetry   time   space   death

Church marquee: AFTER GOOD FRIDAY COMES EASTER
                    GOD ALWAYS WINS

Drive-in marquee: LENTEN SPECIAL
    PO'BOYS   FRIES   DRINK

The men pretty much all have ripped chests

Knitting wasn't really expected

Sign on the weight machine: PUSH TO FAILURE

Whoever becomes a DRUNKARD must be taken to the Whipping Post

Dino's out, he'd like his pictures
Dino blowing smoke out the holes of his beautiful nose

She is *so* sweet you wouldn't believe she had did
    all the things they say she did

That one, she's got a gaggle of tricks up her you-know-what

Drawn on a wall in solitary by a young one
    MOM   LOVE   GOD
    Before he had a face on him

Don't blink don't miss nothing: It's *your* furlough

The Asian lady beetle won't reproduce indoors

The missing girl's father is a probation officer

Do you want to download this
    now   later   no comment

Solitary confinement, Mr. Abbott wrote,
    can alter the ontological makeup of a stone

Mr. Abbott was state-raised; he knows

0% financing and drive-through daiquiris

Baggies of hair and nail clippings entered in

You can bet your nickels

The former 4-term governor will be well-lawyered

What is *your problem*

The tier walker checks on the precariously living

Photographed him with a boner

That's not my pencil, is it

Check his prints:
     plain   tented   looped   burned off

It is a stock dog, the state dog, catahoula
     with the rain-blue eyes

Church marquee: LET'S MEET AT MY HOUSE BEFORE THE GAME

        Lead (kindly) light   Enter (softly) evil

My Dear Conflicted Reader,

   If you will grant me that most of us have an equivocal nature,
and that when we waken we have not made up our minds which direc-
tion we're headed; so that—you might see a man driving to work in a
perfume- and dye-free shirt, and a woman with an overdone tan hold up
an orange flag in one hand, a Virginia Slim in the other—as if this were
their predestination. Grant me that both of them were likely contemplat-
ing a different scheme of things. WHERE DO YOU WANT TO SPEND
ETERNITY the church marquee demands on the way to my boy's school,
SMOKING OR NON-SMOKING. I admit I had not thought of where or
which direction in exactly those terms. The radio ministry says g-o-d has
a wrong-answer button and we are all waiting for it to go off . . .

   Count your grey hairs

   Count your chigger bites

   Count your pills

   Count the times the phone rings

   Count your T cells

   Count your mosquito bites

   Count the days since your last menses

   Count the chickens you've eaten

   Count your cankers

   Count the storm candles

   Count your stitches

   Count your broken bones

   Count the flies you killed before noon

Dear Prisoner,

     I too love.   Faces.   Hands.   The circumference
Of the oaks.   I confess.   To nothing
You could use.   In a court of law.   I found.
That sickly sweet ambrosia of hope.   Unmendable
Seine of sadness.   Experience taken away.
From you.   I would open.   The mystery
Of your birth.   To you.   I know.   We can
Change.   Knowing.   Full well.   Knowing.

                                     It is not enough.

     Poetry   Time   Space   Death
I thought.   I could write.   An exculpatory note.
I cannot.   Yes, it is bitter.   Every bit of it, bitter.
The course taken by blood.   All thinking
Deceives us.   Lead (kindly) light.
Notwithstanding this grave.   Your garden.
This cell.   Your dwelling.   Who is unaccountably free.

               No one promised you the light   or the morrow

Rising, Falling, Hovering

COPPER CANYON PRESS, 2008

Re: Happiness, in pursuit thereof

It is 2005, just before landfall.
Here I am, a labyrinth, and I am a mess.
I am located at the corner of Waterway
and Bluff. I need your help. You will find me
to the left of the graveyard, where the trees
grow especially talkative at night,
where fog and alcohol rub off the edge.
We burn to make one another sing;
to stay the lake that it not boil, earth
not rock. We are running on Aztec time,
fifth and final cycle. Eyes switch on/off.
We would be Mercurochrome to one another
bee balm or chamomile. We should be concrete,
glass, and spandex. We should be digital or,
at least, early. Be ivory-billed. Invisible
except to the most prepared observer.
We will be stardust. Ancient tailings
of nothing. Elapsed breath. No,
we must first be ice. Be nails. Be teeth.
      Be lightning.

from **Rising, Falling, Hovering**

                                             Yesterday

nothing was unusual   a rainy March morning

there were scores of starlings on the ground

she had been thinking about what he said

                        What has been said is said often

Sifting for some interlinear significance   on the pallid grass

the birds   accumulated chromatic density

He stopped her (not vice versa) in the rain to tell her

he had been thinking   the voice beginning to dematerialize

against the slur of cars

                        neither of them moving just yet

In the vapor light of the park

it felt as if the trees were walking with them

as if they had passed into a cloud   she had to ask him

        if this were living or

Never having seen him in fog

which set off his eyes   his voice as spectral

as he looked   his look spectral as neon in fog

The door stuck

on the threshold   electricals on the blink

the curtains eliminated the houses on the hill

cold as mirrors   this rain   wood unwilling to catch

Locked in the time-suck of another

they talked and then fucked and then talked

and fucked and it was like that   grown-up   yet unrehearsed

He would appear central in her book   then go off

on his own   meanwhile   no one but themselves

in the kitchen's recessed lighting   in their underpants

Drinking warm beer   not taking calls

she had no idea   who was calling   kept calling

ringing in the emptiness

I know how you feel   he lied   I know you do

she lied   but to listen   just to listen   tantamount

to forgiveness   it did not matter for what

The longer one lived   the less to forgive

The air changed around them   her face

betrayed her face   she thought more about before

when not much was more than enough

      a pair of cutoffs on a salvaged couch

They wore the scent of smokers then

He rode in front   He said nothing   She drove

He looked out over the water as they crossed the bridge

It was all but dark   he took a pen out of his shirt pocket

and wrote something down

      he cared not to share with her

Her bags had not been in anyone else's possession

Her bracelets set off the metal detector

On the moving sidewalk   she studied his back

through its thin cloth

Him with the scar   do not think him healed

(so the proverb warns)

A funnel of feelings   about going anywhere

during a war

Are your ears popping

trying to make light talk   his half-delineated face

already in twilight   the batting pouring

from clouds below

Were you ever told   the soul detaches from its earthly body

at around 40,000 feet

If they handed you the black box

what would you bequeath

trying to make light talk

He slept with the dead then   nothing roused him

Did she mention a missing spleen   had she warned him

she shaved down there   the night before

One glimpse of the paper was too much

the number of their dead to remain unknown

So the sleepless one hectored the sleeper:

About the other night   I know you are sorry   I am sorry too   We were tired   Me

and my open-shut-case mouth   You and your clockwork disciplines   And I know
         it is

too far to go   But we can't leave it to the forces to rub out the color of the world

What is said has been said before   This is no time for poetry

When the laborer picked up the statue of the santo

    he heard a fluttering and picked a petal off his arm

If the shoes of children are good luck

    what about the boots of a brown-eyed soldier

In his hut the old man loved the mystique of radio

    it took him somewhere irreligious and refrigerated

If they come here he told the much younger woman   Keep still

    make yourself small   make yourself smaller

Posing to look proud on the old burro

    though his mounts had always been thoroughbred

Asked if she had a memory of the camphor-drenched gown

    hung as netting   above the matrimonial hammock

Not really she said   I know I wore it once

    on the other side   al otro lado   and I was smaller then

I have the grey-blue eyes of my gachupín forebears

    but don't take me for one of them

Then: on a certain night and no other

another telegenic war begins.

Can you describe this.

I cannot. This is not the day or the hour.

The color is all wrong.

What dreams I had.

You too.

We were going the speed of night.

We were riding black dogs.

So? What?

So. I don't know.

A plane set down under a bowl of blueness against a ragged ridge. The old
Zapotec town aroused by the onset of evening. The shuttle bus rumbling from airstrip
to zócalo. Swallows silhouetted, then bats against sporadic streetlamps. Lilt of children.
Dogs barking at exhaust pipes. Passport of origin jostled out of mind. Unlit stairs. A worn
lobby off a keyed-up corner. Walls colored by water from a tank of angel fish, the same
ghoulish glow from a muted TV.

Civilian limbs sticking out of wreckage like so much rebar. Baghdad's thirteen-
century chronicle

shelled into the memory hole.

Heat radiating from burning books. Evidence of ago gone.

What has been unloosed cannot be leashed.

What has been stolen will be sold.

From their louvered window on the mezzanine, the stark, darkened hill.
From the roof, view over septic tank of the stark, darkened hill; flounce of
jacaranda in the zócalo.

Who has been torn from one son will be forlorned of another.
These are the sandals that bore the rubbings of
his skin. By this slough, they knew him.

Who has been silenced cannot be unsilenced.

The number of their dead to remain unknown.

Him with the scar   Do not think him healed

¿Mande?

Nada.

¿Mande?

Nada.

to be cont.

One bright night: we will see through the oaths of threat and protection

We will get out of our white cars in our white dresses

We will join the black dogs in a circle of the light

We will turn in the circle of the night

Memory murdered

Not so; instead:

They are spared the television except in passing through the lobby. She struggles with the dailies in Spanish. BÁRBARO ATAQUE: MÁS DE MIL BOMBAS CAYERON EN LA CAPITAL. The headlines transparent. Except on the eternal bottom of the pyramid, expressions of outrage are everywhere, except on the bottom where hunger numbs even anger.

In Mexico's capital, which is teeming, which is sinking by inches, which is ringed by cardboard colonias, which are teeming, the day after the bombs have begun to drop on Baghdad, the florists are bringing their blooms to the heart, de costumbre, on Fridays, to the hotels and restaurants, the markets and sidewalk vendors.

And this Friday, no different, except the bombs are blooming in Baghdad, and in the heart of the capital of Old Mexico, which is sinking, the florists deliver to the zócalo, forming a quiet convoy, which stops traffic for miles, and the florists unload in early quiet, first light.

They empty their pungent cargo and begin to make a mosaic, which can be read by the guests in the Gran Hotel and the Majestic, which spells NO A LA GUERRA Y SÍ A LA PAZ. And the blooms left over which are given away to passersby.

And in Oaxaca City, on the roof of their hotel, looking over the zócalo: papier-mâché effigies, calla lilies, vigil by candle, graffiti on the walls of the gringo watering hole, and a wasted apparition circling the center, panhandling for smokes.

And in the following days the taxi drivers head for the Alameda, in Mexico City, flying pennants of peace from their aerials, and traffic, which is teeming, is stopped for miles. All quiet in the capital of the old Aztec empire. Silence in the heart, habitat of 22,000,000 souls, which is sinking by centimeters. Which in inches equals eight a year.

End Thoughts

In the beginning the usual dark dark of very dark
In a few years there appears a crack in the dark a very small crack
The crack as I said appears very small
        and jagged as cracks are

The temperature has already been adjusted
        by the state
Our obsolescence built into the system

When you use the ladies' room
        do not put your purse on the floor
When the civilian words are dispensed
        different meanings will be assigned
The new meanings will be fired
        at the head and groin area

For instance saying Can't a girl get anything to eat around here
would now signify Water with a stomach wound is fatal
Or if you were to say The mariachis are coming
        it would be interpreted as Just open the f__g trunk

All extroverted activity will be suspended
        in residential zones
Absolutely no tea parties under the trees

Crying helps
Crying doesn't help

One wants to make oneself smaller than the mouse
under the icebox One wants to dry into invisible ink

One has a sense of something out there that needs saving
        and one ought to attach the buckle
to a heavy-gauge wire and pull him through

Waking up knowing this much is not the hard part
nor lifting the head from its existential drift
      it's the sticking of one's foot off the edge
      lowering it to the cold floor

and finding the correct instrument
to work that crack into a big enough opening
      to venture forward

Before the fall no story after the fall the old story
After the fires floods along with serpents and bugs
After the floods years of drought
After drought just dusk which is when everything
      really begins to hurt

      and then there is the human dimension

One With Others [a little book of her days]

COPPER CANYON PRESS, 2010

Some names were changed or omitted in light of the interpretive nature of this account. Others because they still live there. People may have been rendered as semblances and composites of one another. And others, spoken into being. Memories have been tapped, and newspapers consulted. Books referenced. Times fused and towns overlaid. This is not a work of history. It is a report full of holes, a little commemorative edition, and it aspires to the borrowed-tuxedo lining of fiction. In the end, it is a welter of associations.

Up and down the towns in the Delta, people were stirring. Cotton was right about shoe top. Daylilies hung from their withering necks. Temperatures started out in the 90s with no promise of a good soaking. School was almost out. The farm bells slowly rang for freedom. The King lay moldering in the ground over a year. The scent of liberation stayed on, but it was hard to bring the trophy home. Hard to know what came next; one thing, and one thing only was known, no one wanted to go home dragging their tow sack; no one wanted to go home empty-handed.

Over at the all-Negro junior high, a popular teacher has been fired for "insubordination" for a "derogatory" letter he wrote the superintendent saying the Negro has no voice. No voice at all. It was the start of another cacophonous summer.

*

FAMILY OF V'S BABYSITTER: Another stifling day in Big Tree. There was a fight on the South Side, a family disturbance that got loud, got ugly. Cops came. There were arrests. Her father went to the jailhouse to find out about his sons. They wouldn't tell him anything. They wouldn't let him post bail. He got a call late that night. The sons were going to be released. He went down there. In the a.m. hours they let them go. First they cut the outside lights. A line of pickups were idling in the lot. The men in the trucks, the patriarch knew them all. They were from the farms. He was the flat-fixer for every one of those farms. They said they were going to take them to a fish fry. It was a [N-word] fry. That's what it was. They beat her father. Beat the crap out of him. The youngest boys ran off. One jumped from the overpass. His knees jammed. Permanently. The brothers scrambled under a vehicle in a carport. The patriarch hid in the sticker bushes. He couldn't see. He bled until he blacked out.

Maybe the reverend knew they were under his vehicle. Maybe he didn't. He held his tongue. It was a choreographed release. Don't you see. The police notified the men on the farms, the Night Riders, gave them time to get together. The flat-fixer knew every one of them. And they knew him.

✝ ✝ ✝

VIETNAM VETERAN, RETIRED NURSE: We were in the second wave of arrests. We met at the funeral home and broke into groups of fourteen. That way we were legal. A lot of us still got arrested and transported in horse trailers to the dressing room of the pool. Took three of us in the dogcatcher wagon.

I was eighteen. Graduated and went to Vietnam. Wounded. Purple Heart. Came home and town under curfew.

I picked my mother up from church. My car was surrounded. A woman held a brick. She saw I had a Service .45. I said, Lady, you hit my car . . .
Hardest part to come back and see signs that said [N-word].

All my kids were military. Oldest son killed by police officer in Memphis. Had a great job, went to church, great family. Now the cop is dead. He was black too.

Jesus saved me from the hatred. It's the only way.

When life gets you down / keep looking up

163

✠ ✠ ✠

RETIRED WELDING TEACHER: Kept first watch on the porch with the lights off. Wore my fatigues. Holding a rifle. Since Nam, we were armed, too.

That's when things began to calm down. When both sides were armed. Black people coming back from the Mekong delta toting M16s, the way we used to walk off the fields with hoes.

There was a shooting at the Tastee-Freez. Things got too dangerous and kind of chilled off.

A teacher has been fired for a derogatory letter, for insubordination in which he told the superintendent the Negro had no voice.

It was a riot, a rampage. An outbreak. A disturbance. The students called it a boycott, a walkout. Gentle Reader, it was an uprising.

During the morning of this date, no one had been given any cause to believe that a riot was imminent. However the superintendent had notified the

164

chief of the firing of a teacher at the all-Negro junior high and had stated that there might be trouble.

The first teacher to approach the study hall after the disturbance began was not on hall duty but went on the basis of a report that there was trouble.

When he arrived there was not another teacher in the study hall. The students were then in the process of overturning tables and throwing chairs.

The students, by this time numbering in the hundreds, went out upon the grounds; some or all of them continued their course of conduct throwing bottles, rocks, or other objects at the building resulting in breakage of glass.

A bottle or some other object struck an assistant superintendent on the forehead inflicting a moderately severe wound requiring medical attention.

WE [the grand jury] are aware that every effort is being made to bring about better facilities, yet we feel that this alone will not cure the ills that exist. Whether it be crowded conditions, lack of discipline, lack of respect, political and/or social ills, or imagined political or social ills, none of these excuse or

justify damage and destruction of our education institutions.

Immediate Steps

Must Be Taken

Toward More Strict

Position Of Discipline,

Respect, Order

Quickly As Possible

Closer Observation

Take Whatever Steps

Necessary

Bring It

Immediately

Under Control

Protect Property

Rights Of Those

Desiring

Deserving

Opportunity

Education

Our County Judge

Doing Excellent Job

[later sent up for racketeering]

Under Circumstances

Best Crime Deterrent

Sure Detection

Swift Apprehension

Certain Punishment

Testimony Shows

An Excess Of $19,000

Spent Restoring

The Building

To Habitable Condition

A month later it was unofficially reported that a walkout was in progress at the all-Negro senior high.

Langston's word was *fester.*

King's was *thingification. The thingification of our humanity.*

What the King called *nobodiness.*

Festina lente, with all deliberate speed, make haste slowly. Voluntary gradualism, glacial time.

THE DA said it was not in the public interest to bargain with any evildoers; they had no cause to meet with or make concessions to any bush-league agitators from Little Rock, nor for that matter, with any hoodlum parasite element.

He spoke he claimed for the judge, the sheriff, the city, and himself.

THE CHIEF [former bouncer at the Cotton Club]: They got to yeah-yeahing each other. The whites have taken it off of them until they've got tired of it.

THE CONCERNED CITIZENS COUNCIL's first guest speaker [over cookies and punch at their new offices in the former city barbershop]: The rule of the majority is being eroded by the minority.

MAYOR: I don't think they have any real grievance.

COUNTY JUDGE: I assure you we've been nothing but good to the [N-word].

Come again.

You've got me, man, said the Invader to his assailants.

You've got me. [It was not part of his plan to die in Arkansas.]

THE PUBLISHER says this community has no quarrel with its Negro citizens, to the contrary, the average white and Negro citizen in Big Tree get along as well as citizens in any city anywhere in the world; the problem lies in the hands of a small minority of troublemakers who seem hell-bent on making Big Tree a focal point of racial unrest. The time for pacifying them is past. Our officials have no alternative now but to meet them head-on.

HEAD OF THE BIRCHERS [that backdoor abortionist] told newsmen [over cookies and punch] that the president was leading the nation toward insolvency, surrender, and socialism.

DEAR ABBY,

My daughter married a 30-year-old mama's boy who is in love with tropical fish. He has 13 tanks of them. Just to give you an idea he paid $14 for 1 little fish.

DEAR MOTHER,

Water seeks its own level—even in a fish tank.

What's your problem.

Lions cancel annual picnic due to concerns.

Spinster luncheon honors fiancée [an attractive blond]

of Mr. Peacock.

County board recommends dismissal of Negro caseworker.

Death of a Gunfighter ends Wednesday.

ELSEWHERE:

Camille pummels Gulf.

Israeli jets attack Egypt.

Squads ready to break up Irish riots.

Sept 3 marks the death of Ho.

✠ ✠ ✠

Harry says, What we really want from our time on this planet, is *that which is not this,* we want *the ethical this;* we want to feel and transmit.

It is known that when a blackbird calls in the marsh, all sound back and if one note is missing all take notice. This is the solidarity we are born to.

King said no one could be an outsider who lived inside these borders. There are no Invaders.

What the white man wanted, no less than complete control.

171

Who expected the sidewalks cleared when they came down them [as in the days of the Raj].

✠ ✠ ✠

The boys hid under the reverend's vehicle. I can't say if the reverend knew they were there. I can't say if he didn't know. He probably knew. They hid on the concrete slab under the block. They held their breath and listened. One of them was hurt pretty bad. And the patriarch, the flat-fixer, lost an eye.

Hateful words survive in sticky clumps

Furry thoughts skid across the yellow line

And over the muddy embankment.

Big enough to hunt, being hunted.

Says the sheriff, Nowadays you can't

Even say chigger you have to say Cheegro.

They fired the flat-fixer. They fired him after they put out his eye. The eel

in the L'Anguille never were. The flat-fixer who said he'd get the radio fixed. He

knew who could fix it. They fired him. Never held an eel, she just slithered. The

fixer, they said, stole their shortwave. He had it fixed. They fired him. But first

they put out his eye. So they named it L'Anguille. And the Mississippi receives

them both, but you wouldn't notice now. It's casino to casino from here to the

Big Easy. The other river, that would be the St. Francis.

They said they would take this harm. They would take it this time, would

move on. They would walk away, walk away. Turn a blind eye. They would

go forward into the seasons of their lives. They would see the sun shiver as

it disappeared behind willow and cottonwood, the blackbird threading the

phone lines, the combine continuing to rust on its haunches. They would not be

deformed by this hatefulness. Nor be comforted by religion [though would be

their women]. But if anyone ever touched any of them ever again. They would put this town on the map. They made their pact. They took the no-quarter oath. They were eight men strong. And they meant it, Gentle Reader. They meant it.

Outside of North Little Rock they are joined by a Quaker.

From ONE TOO YOUNG TO JOIN THE UPRISING: The all-Negro elementary school was behind the all-Negro junior high. They were letting us out early. The troopers were there. We wanted to see. We wanted to see the goings-on. I got to watch a couple of chairs fly out the window is all. And here come my loving mother to keep her baby out of harm's way.

THE RETIRED WELDING TEACHER: After they put us in the pool, they taunted us. With chimp chants. They brought a TV and set it up and made us watch Tarzan. They wouldn't let us sleep. They made us watch.

ONE OF THE STUDENTS ARRESTED AND PUT IN THE POOL: They arrested us in the morning and drove us around until dark. They told us all kind of things. But we didn't know what they were going to do with us. The last thing my mother said before I left the house—Don't you get in that line. Don't you get in that line, girl. Stay away. Remain calm. I won't even come see you if you go to jail. But later I found out she did try to see me. They gave us hand-me-down books. Turn to page 51, the teacher would say. It would be torn out. Lunch was slabs of butter between two pieces of bread. Milk usually spoiled and it cost 2¢.

GRADUATE OF ALL-WHITE HIGH SCHOOL, First Year of Choice: You have to understand about my mom, if she calls us up at three in the morning, and says she wants ice cream, you get dressed and go buy ice cream. Even if you have to drive to Memphis. If she says talk to this woman, you talk.

Teachers' kids stuck together. We were the only ones with a telephone, a TV, a record player.

Blew the front of our house off the day before my father's funeral.

I see someone from that school now and think, I wonder if your father is still alive and if he is still wearing his little Klan outfit on Saturday night.

All of us who went to the white school have a story. Houlie went to Liberia. My husband never went back in the building.

HER MOTHER: I accept nothing less than respect. You hear me.

I haven't seen the lightning bugs yet but I do enjoy them. And by day I enjoy the butterflies. I sit on my step; they flutter around me. And I think, well maybe somebody is paying me a visit.

A teacher sent a note home saying she couldn't understand my oldest daughter. I told her I curse better than you speak. My daughter is not going to flunk English because you cannot speak it. No less than respect, you get what I'm saying.

The department store hired a couple of light-skinned blacks to work in the back [Saturdays only].

I remember her. Bought an Emerson from her husband for the Big Shootout.

Parents came down with food for the kids when we found out where they were. Police threw the burgers over the fence.

The former legislator said he fished with a man who told him the school

wouldn't be there when he came to teach in the fall, first year of Choice.

They march along here, the military road

The road they walk built by humpers

Those were the Irish

They pass Blackfish Lake

Ditch #1 about where they crossed

Gerstaecker slept here bundled up in a buffalo's skin

But first the Choctaw Removal; then came the Creek with ponies;

Then Chickasaw; then Cherokee, maybe Sequoyah among them his

syllabary nearly finished

Now stood another anonymous racist calling them names

His rod extended / his line hung up in his own ignominy

THE MAN IMPORTED FROM MEMPHIS: When you get change you

keep pushing and you get more. The hardest thing is to get the ball rolling.

We are marching to get this fear out of your hearts. You must remember

the white man puts his pants on the same way you do, one leg at a time.

Since I have been involved with the Movement I have not committed any

so-called crime.

The Movement is the best thing I've ever been involved in. It channeled my

energy into constructive efforts.

My aunt raised me. She worked as a domestic for the family of Judge Bailey Brown.

If white people can ride down their highways with guns, I can walk down the highway unarmed.

Old enough to hunt, hunted.

When people have anticipated something and they have been let down, you must find some way to let them use up this excess energy. [That, Gentle Reader, is the accursed share.]

My walk will help do this for the people of Arkansas. Not a question of violence or nonviolence. Survival is the point. We are going to survive one way or the other. Sweet Willie Wine, V, and the Invaders are

Walking we are just walking

Dead doe on the median

Whoever rides into the scene changes it

Pass a hickory dying on the inside

A black car that has not moved for years

Forever forward / backward never

The Poet, the Lion, Talking Pictures, El Farolito, a Wedding in St. Roch, the Big Box Store, the Warp in the Mirror, Spring, Midnights, Fire & All

COPPER CANYON PRESS, 2016

In a Word,
a World

I love them all.

I love that a handful, a mouthful, gets you by, a satchelful can land you a job, a well-chosen clutch of them could get you laid, and that a solitary word can initiate a stampede, and therefore can be formally outlawed—even by a liberal court bent on defending a constitution guaranteeing unimpeded utterance. I love that the Argentine gaucho has over two hundred words for the coloration of horses and the Sami language of Scandinavia has over a thousand words for reindeer based on age, sex, appearance—e.g., a *busat* has big balls or only one big ball. More than the pristine, I love the filthy ones for their descriptive talent as well as transgressive nature. I love the dirty ones more than the minced, in that I respect extravagant expression more than reserved. I admire reserve, especially when taken to an ascetic *n*th. I love the particular lexicons of particular occupations. The substrate of those activities. The nomenclatures within nomenclatures. I am of the unaccredited school that believes animals did not exist until Adam assigned them names. My relationship to the word is anything but scientific; it is a matter of faith on my part, that the word endows material substance, by setting the thing named apart from all else. *Horse,* then, unhorses what is not horse.

My American Scrawl

Increasingly indecisive, about matters both big and little, I have found that poetry is the one arena where I am not inclined to crank up the fog machine, to palter or dissemble or quaver or hastily reverse myself. This is the one scene where I advance determined, if not precisely ready, to do battle with what an overly cited Jungian described as the anesthetized heart, the heart that does not react.

Poems are my building projects. I inhabit them for the time it takes to have every corner lit, and then I clear out, taking what I think I need to start over. Invariably I have forgotten something I could really use; so I have to make do or figure out an unfamiliar, irregular means to make the next structure. Sometimes I work in discrete units; other times I work on an extended complex. Less and less am I persuaded by the medium's essence, and more and more I am pulled by its mutability. In recent years I have worked on various projects with photographer Deborah Luster. We are both restless in our processes, and stable in our sensibilities. We are both interested in exploring the possible ways by which you can make meaningful contact with a consciousness other than your own without surrendering the possibilities to an obvious common ground. Ideally the result will be spacious, fierce, strange, homey, humorous, tragic, etc., etc., an Earth station where almost anything can take place. More are welcome than can fit inside. I am not averse to torching a place that is not habitable (so long as no one is inside). I will uncover a use for the ashes.

In a Word,
a World

I know the adjective can be a nuisance, and the adverb clumsy. I am a touch sick of the poetic inflation around prepositions. I would prefer that conjunctions were less visibly functional. Articles can clutter. The verb works the hardest. It should be the best paid. And I know fifteenth letter *O* is the best of all: O my black frying pan. O my fallen arches. O my degenerating fibroids. O what's the point. O little man at the foot of my bed, please don't steal my pillow.

In a Word,
a World

Although I take a special pleasure in compounds, whether or not they have been duly authorized—*silverback, deepstep, lovegreen, pothead, eyestring, closeburn, shirttail, boneman, wristwatch*—no words please me so much as the one- or two-syllable noun. It appears at its best left unaccompanied by an article. At its best, shed of adjective. Whether it is singular or plural matters. I prefer *hours* to *hour* and *roads* to *road; hills* to *hill, faces* to *face,* but also *fish* to *fishes* and *tooth* to *teeth.* Does it matter whether I know the reason. Or that I can but vaguely supply one. Probably, but the reasons hop around, and seem purely personal. Writing is choosing. Choosing is decision-making. Decisions among word choices are among the most delectable of the whole writing experience. They may be accidental, they may be serendipitous. Never arbitrary. Decisions are being made. Even when subliminal. An accurate computation of the decisions involved in composing a poem of three–five lines would be an Oulipian challenge. I like the weight, I like the lilt, I like the scene. I don't like the *s* here but do not mind it there. I like the noun to situate hue. A gourd is gourd-colored. It's extra if its sound value complements its substance, say, for example, *hock.* (Whereas *God* is just very odd.) And optimal when much of its -*ness*–ness as possible is thought held in its common name. On the other hand, there's an off-kiltering pleasure in discovering that words do not mean what you might think they would: *debridement,* for instance; *adumbrate, disinterest, enervate,* and *nonplussed* are frequent tripper-uppers.

The not knowing whether what you've set down is any good

You don't, you never know, as his lordliness the besotted John Berryman told an ingenue, the parson's son W.S. Merwin. If you have to know, don't write. Frankly, if you are easily satisfied with your efforts, it is probably too facile a task for you. If it does not push and pull you to the frontiers of what you know, and then on to where the really good stuff—all that you do not know—is, you need a more strenuous challenge. Something that really blows your knees out. The painter Ed Ruscha is reported by Dave Hickey to have claimed, "Bad art is 'Wow! Huh?' Good art is 'Huh? Wow!'" That pretty much hits the spot for me.

Poetry is hard to abuse except by writing it poorly, and then the damage, face it, is finite.

In a Word, a World

I also admit a weakness for prefixes over suffixes, *un-* in particular because I favor the negative: *unbegotten, unforgiven, unhorsed.* Whereas -*ism*s are too ideological and -*itis*es too pathological. Some words should be said more than once for their effect, *river river.* Said once, it quickly shivers and stops. Seconded, it begins to flow. A word is chosen and put into position, for particular effect. It is tantamount to hauling a big rock, carrying it a great distance, and setting it down, only to realize it should not be occupying that spot in this circumstance. It is dead on arrival but you barely have the reserves to move it again. Although if not moved, and best before darkness spreads, it will create a hole commensurate with its heft, and it will encroach on the tender shoots of words nearby. If, however, it was the exact word you wanted and rightly lodged, the satisfaction is granted, on-the-spot, so to speak. And the entire surround is enhanced. Then, there is its commonly attendant ability to convert its stationariness into action. One can truck on over to that enormous rock and rock it out of the hole it is beginning to create for itself. I rock, you rock, one trucks.

My American Scrawl

Poetry requires movement in its direction, faith in its persistence, receptivity to its fundamental worthwhileness. Within its unanesthetized chambers there is quite a commotion going on. Choices have to be made with respect to every mark. Not every mistake should be erased. Nor shall the unintelligible be left out. Order is there to be macheted from the tangles of words. Results are impossible to measure. A clearing is drawn around the perimeter as if by a crooked stick with a crooked nail on the end.

In a Word,
a World

I love the nouns of a time in a place, where a sack once was a poke and native skag was junk glass not junk and junk was just junk not smack and smack entailed eating with your mouth open, and an Egyptian one-eye was an egg, sunny-side up, and a nation sack was a flannel amulet, worn only by women, to be touched only by women, especially around Memphis. Red sacks for love and green for money. Of course the qualifying adjective *nation* does exercise an otherwise uneventful noun.

In a Word,
a World

I like nouns that go up: *loft.* And ones that sink: *mud.* I like the ones that peck: *chicken.* And canter: *canter.* Those that comfort: *flannel* and *pelt. Cell* is an excellent word, in that it sweetly fulfills its assigned sound in a small, thin container. Unlike *hell,* which is disappointing. Overall. Wanting in force and fury. I like that a lone syllable names a necessary thing: *bridge, house, door, food, bed.* And the ones that sustain us: *dirt, milk,* and so on. What a thing, that a syllable—*birth, time, space, death*—points to the major mysteries with such simplicity, as with a silent finger. And to our very vital parts: *head, snout, heart, butt.* And our fundamental feeling: *fear.*

In a Word,
a World

The mother word, word of words, must pull everything in range to its skin if not its core. It must set one's head awhirling. It must whelm the mouth when spoken, and clobber the senses when confronted. It must include everyone everywhere. Forever. And so, *world*, Middle English, from the Old English *weorold,* also appearing as *warld, wardle, werld, worlde, worold, woruld, wurld, wuruld*—that's the word for me. Such surround-sound amplitude, such magnetic force. It cannot be got outside of. One must hew to its basic requirements or succumb to its anguish. "World. World. O world!" Made of everything and nothing.

Questionnaire in January

Colette said writing leads only to writing. Where does it lead you. And what led you here.

To what mark are you attempting to hold yourself.

What do poets talk about. What do they have to talk about.

Into what forms do you see poetry pouring, morphing, shuddering.

Is there anything you see that poetry has the capacity to alter or altogether upend.

Agnes Martin said, of painting *White Flower,* she was trying to express the emotions we feel when we see grey geese descending.

Can you put words to an inchoate desire.

René Char writes, What can we do to bring the ship nearer to its longing.

Margaret Avison says poetry results when every word is written in the full light of all a writer knows.

Can you fix anything. Anything at all.

Could a score be organized around your writing. Can you describe its shape. Can you describe its sound.

Does a voice apply to your thoughts distinct from talking.

In your memory, with what smell do you associate most powerfully. Evan Lavender-Smith writes, There are certain smells that have the power to dissolve the problem of life. . . . Sophia's head sweat.

If your goal was to forget yourself in your writing, what would you foreground in your stead.

James Hillman said, Get out of history, get into geography. What do you say.

Are you possessed by a topophilia. (The feeling of affection that individuals have for particular places, a term introduced by W.H. Auden, 1947. Places in this sense may vary in scale from a single room to a nation or continent. Topophilia is an important aspect of the symbolic meaning and significance of landscapes.)

Is the goal of community attainable through the gates of poetry.

Marianne Moore wrote of poetry: I, too, dislike it. Reading it, however, with a perfect contempt for it, one discovers in it, after all, a place for the genuine. What do you say.

Frank O'Hara said poetry is as useful as a machine. How so.

Beckett said the form must let the mess in.

Can you say something about the architecture of a poem.

About the visual plane.

What if a line were just something to which you arbitrarily added a virgule.

What is your area of "research."

What is your favorite body of water and why.

Identify a pattern in something other than a poem which you might apply to a poem. It could be an evacuation route, a small-town phone book, a crazy quilt, a roulette wheel, a menu, a ship's manifest, etc., etc.

Try composing a rhapsody on a single word.

Have you any tenets.

What is missing from your writing now.

How softly can you play.

Do you have an identifiable palette. (If you don't know what color to take, take black. Picasso.)

Picasso said to always work against, even against oneself, and Morton Feldman said he worked by negation.

Your thoughts on the "career" of poetry.

In what regard to your life do you hold your poetry.

Genine Lentine writes of her process:
>I let the leaves
>come to the branch
>and when the bee is at the
>blossom, I listen.

And about drought:
>I spread my root hairs and wait.

What is your physical experience of poetry.

What commands your attention.

Something about nouns.

Do you approve of eggplant.

In *Practical Water*, in partial response to her own question as to what it is to live a moral life, Brenda Hillman writes, "An ethics occurs at the edge / of what we know / / The creek goes underground about here." I am forced to consider my own example, greyer than my father's.

Roots aside, do you see yourself as having alignments, alliances, well-delineated antipathies, a sense of what you are in apposition with and opposition to as a writer.

Emily Dickinson said poetry was her letter to the world. Write me.

I read this poem in some magazine without writing down the poet's name. It pleased me, the second stanza esp.:

> *from* DREADLOCKS
>> *for Jean-Michel Basquiat*

> All the colors
> wired together
> so when he
> combs his hair
> the train explodes.

> (Years later I uncovered the attribution: Elaine Equi.)

Does weather matter to poetry. Is it always night. Can we count on a sluggish ooze of light. Dream's mildew.

Linda Norton wrote that she "walked into poetry / in search of a place to rest, / a place to suffer formally"; Jack Gilbert remarked that poetry helps you to suffer more efficiently. Some comfort can be found in that.

Does poetry protect anything from anyone or any one from any thing.

Water seeks to get in as does poetry. True or false.

Compose a self-portrait in fewer than 12 lines. Fewer than 9. Fewer than 3.

Simone Weil wrote that a mind enclosed in language is in prison.

Apply a crèche, an exaltation, a float, a skein, or smack of adjectives to your poetry.

Returning to this matter of form, Czesław Miłosz said that form in poetry has many uses; one of them is, like refrigeration, to preserve bad meat. Think of better uses. Be specific.

"If not a writer, then I would probably be a geologist. I majored in geology, was heading to graduate school in paleontology, and then the doe-eyed dark angel touched my shoulder with a finger and the doctor said, third-stage melanoma, let's go. In no time, I'd lost my spleen, a line of lymph nodes, a bear's mouthful of flesh and muscle over my shoulder blade, and a rectangle of skin, about the size of a City Lights paperback, that had been stripped for use as a graft. Lying in the hospital, nothing but words in my head, I began to imagine another way to love the earth, and to find something to stand on," wrote Forrest Gander in response to the question, If not a writer . . .

Even if it is nothing except fishes, on what will you stand.

So my singing nemesis, where do we go from here.

Thinking of an Arthur Sze poem that opens,
　　　"Fuck you, *fuck you*," he repeated as he drove down the dirt road
　　　　　　while tamarisk branches scraped the side of the pickup;

I wonder why I take such pleasure in that invective. In this case it partly has to do with what soon follows, including the synesthetic,
　　　　　　who hears a night-blooming cereus
　　　　　　unfold a white blossom by the windowsill?

199

I like a high contrast, and he is particularly prone to pulling that off, though this is just one of scores of his examples.

Do you want to tell me a secret.

When you feel that gravitational pull, release your fleet of dreams.

Do you prefer warmer or cooler, blended or bent tones.

Matthew Arnold said that at bottom poetry is a criticism of life. Do you agree this is a function of the art. What then. Give reasons.

Anthocyanins make a beech leaf purple and strawberries red. Though vertebrates do not contain the pigment, what makes you so blue. Granted, color is subjective.

Grandma Wright completed fourth grade; the school year was
under 100 days; I don't know how far she walked to attend; I
know her trousseau was composed of rough, simple cloth, including
laundered, folded, and bleached flour sacks; I know she raised five sons and acres
and acres of tomatoes;
her husband Robert and a son drove the tomatoes to Eureka Springs in a wagon
and sold them for $8 a ton; the favorite son, the bright, blue-eyed, wavy-haired blond
Audie, was shot down over southern Italy in 1943;
he and my brilliant,
honorable father Ernie Edward had planned to open a law office together after
the war,
and no family member ever fully recovered from Audie's death. If the one-room house
still stands, the hillside is overtaken by thorn trees, and the peonies Grandmother Wright
planted as a young bride. This was the only record LuVindie Wright, née a Williams,
chronicled in her Self-Pronouncing New Testament; it is
my favorite found poem:

End Sheet

Harley Wright oprated on Ap 23, 1966

Ernie Wright and Aline Collins was married Friday Aug 22, 1941

Noah that built the ark was 950 years old when he died

Hot water heater was put in Jan 18, 1954

ShallCross

COPPER CANYON PRESS, 2016

Light Bulb Poem

at 4 o'clock I am at the door
with a bare hand of snow
laughing shamelessly
I undo my shirt
we'll pick up at the next chapter
my beloved are the words
of the rambler
if not the words the substance
the snow smeared across my front
warm to the touch
though we remain separated
as if by a chair
and I unwilling to read ahead

Amarillo Poem

A room across from a sporting house. With the dark,
I watched a woman washing the men off; then herself
she washed with a different cloth. It was fall. I was sitting
on my bed in my flame-proof gown. Every morning
I had to jump aboard my suitcase to get it to close.

Poem with Some Water Damage

She kept boarders kept hens
in the heart of town
heard birds whenever I phoned
now bullhorn now chopper
someone puts a plate in her hands
hours later someone takes the plate
from her hands *Damn* he says
if it isn't overcast again

Poem with a Dead Tree

it is late afternoon
she avoids looking
in its direction
she can feel
it moving toward her
in shaky black lines

Poem from the End of Old Wire Road

hands as heavy as rocks
in the pockets of a Goodwill coat
kicking up leaves
she uncovers four trout lilies
Ah spring how it made her
want to walk backwards
or stick a fork in her side

Breathtaken

i.

napping   in her car with her 19-week fetus

at the tattoo parlor   behind the barber shop

in a coffee-colored shotgun, Seventh Ward   a triple

                                   one of the men wore women's clothes

in the chest by a neighbor

under a cell tower

during a concert at Hush

next to a snowball stand

in a trash bin   facedown

in the shadow of the Superdome

facedown   she brought a flower to the spot

in the driver's seat

fleeing   into Sleepy's Lounge

while walking down Chippewa, 8:20 p.m.

                                              she had on the dress he bought her

facedown

bringing back stuff to make gumbo

lying on his back on Willow   watching the dark torsos of clouds shots sprayed from a green van

working on a house   he loved his mother's pies

by his idling car

faceup   watching the clouds bulk up and blow over

in the passenger seat on Sister Street

walking home, 5:25 p.m.   carrying a bottle of whole milk

in a room at the Travelodge   pending identification

in the family living room   watching his program

parked in his pickup   half a muffuletta in his lap

beneath a tree   looking up through a canopy of speckled light

in a pile of debris   outside a blighted house

faceup   the sun severed by rebar

after being carjacked the night before   his girlfriend

after they raped her they shot her   Hush

one spoke   through a slot in his stockinet

inside his apartment   in his favorite shirt

from a black Acura

felled on Constance

while changing a flat on I-10 eastbound

in the stairwell   of an Algiers complex on Josephine on Christmas night   a double

on the sidewalk on St. Ann   wearing counterfeit Nikes

facedown   he tried to avoid the cracks in the walk

beside a bicycle   a thin chevron of hair above the lip

side entrance of St. Luke's

last seen leaving a club   in the Sugar District

inside his water-damaged apartment   a witness

to a murder trial postponed

                    [first the killer had to drop off his kids]

ii.

corner of Hollygrove and Palm

over the Industrial Canal on Chef Menteur

lying on Olive Street   looking at the moon

swollen, urinous

inside a silver Isuzu

corner of Touro and N. Roman

at the former Sugar Bowl Lanes   decomposed

near Elysian Fields overpass

in the backyard   watching the rags of cloud float over

driving north

driving a black Buick Regal

driving on Felicity

on the sidewalk about noon

                                                                    clouds

pushing past   the lenses of his Ray-Bans

in the courtyard of a housing complex   near the struggling live oak

N. Roman again   hushed

inside a red Chevy Lumina

in the Community Care   Psychiatric Hospital

after being stomped and beaten   and forsaken

facing   a mud nest under a gallery

on Dauphine

in the backyard   wearing counterfeit True Religion jeans

in the front yard

Calyisse, 19, and Fitzgerald, 19

                                                 in an abandoned house near Fig Street

in Gert Town   home of Blue Plate Mayonnaise Factory

                                                                    elevation 0

iii.

[*Fabulous,* that was her byword]

inside a black Toyota Scion

inside her ransacked house

inside Happy Jack Social and Pleasure Club

lying in the street   facing

                                        a deflated basketball under a parked car

iv.

N. Prieur again

in his FEMA trailer   asleep with the TV on

in the Tallowtree neighborhood

inside his home with his throat slit

                                        [by gunshot unless otherwise noted]

in his house on Terpsichore

on Claiborne at the line   between Pigeon Town and Hollygrove

New Year's Day

                            in front of his grandmother's house, Sixth Ward

shot 14 times   [courtesy of NOPD] at a graduation party in the backyard

                                        a girl totally in love with poetry

mother of a 30-month-old   the father ambushed in his car

a few days after she learned she was pregnant

he never even knew   [her cycle was off]

by men in black   coming out from the trees shooting

in a car chase

sprawled   out of a black Chevrolet Monte Carlo

twins   on Telemachus and Baudin

under a vehicle   from a beating

intersection of Conti and Treme

in the Holy Cross neighborhood

in Le Petit Motel   an unidentified woman

in the 8200 block of Chef Menteur

at Cooper public housing

next to an abandoned complex in St. Roch   [found by a dog]

at Cooper public housing again   his mama is going to miss him

something awful

on Elysian Fields

on Touro again

found in her pickup

former NOPD   near Downman Rd. ramp

in a baby blue Volkswagen   talking

through the car window   smoke gushing out of her nostrils

at Iberville again

in the back of the head   near The Commons Bar

in a Cardinals cap

homeless, stabbed in torso

homeless, stabbed in back

on Loyola

on Danzinger Bridge, a boy, 17   in the back [NOPD]

on Danzinger Bridge, a man, mentally challenged

                                                    in the back [NOPD again]

behind the wheel of his new car

by a peer, 14

on Babylon Street, 17, by peers

in Gert Town   elevation 0

home to Blue Plate Mayonnaise Factory

playing dice on the porch   a triple

three more still breathing   Lower Ninth

Jack's Bus Stop

near the Super Sunday parades

in town to visit relatives for Memorial Day

                                when he stayed in Houston

he was out of the woods   so his mama thought

in Terrytown   named for the developer's first girlchild, a triple

near intersection of Old Gentilly Rd.

                     and Michoud, found beside the road

Brittany, 17   [who never met a stranger]

the baby would not stop crying

                 multiple fractures and rends in the anus

in the Ninth Ward, a double

in St. Roch near intersection of Johnson   and Music

N. Claiborne and Frenchmen

Wendy a bartender at Aunt Tiki's and   Starlight by the Park

corner of Governor Nicholls and Dauphine   by three teens

[turned in by the parents]

his shredded heart   feeling death upon him

the evidence voluminous

I put her body in water I'm willing to give

                                        you that the prisoner replied

That other, that's a grey area

[he was said to get off watching

                                        their eyes roll to the back of their head]

a preponderance of evidence requires   a lower standard than proof

beyond a reasonable doubt

once you start talking about   more than one murder

and the defendant is ugly to look at

                                        ugly acting or has an ugly history

in water   evidence such as semen

can be ruined by marine life

the Handcuff Muzzle™ is an effective

                                        and versatile restraint device

the Handcuff Muzzle™ is made of   vented mesh nylon

                                        [this material has a long life expectancy]

this material is washable and comes   in a variety of colors

the Grommet guarantees a snug fit

in two main sizes   one is for securing females or males

with smaller hands

the other size   your general population an X-large bag   by special order

the Wrap is the ultimate immobilization system

[never think upwards   unless downwards first]

it's police blotter time   Did you lock the side door

                                                       Well, I said, Hell to yes

v.

inside a white Chevy Impala

in the rear of Fischer public housing complex

on the side of abandoned Kennedy High

lying in an alley next to an abandoned house   faceup

                                                       dreaming of electric sheep

vi.

hushed   in a robbery

in a struggle   with a man

being questioned   [that was Cotton]

inside Exclusive Cuts   [Consuelo]

run down by a car driven   by his daughter's boyfriend

in a rented Pontiac

in New Edition Bar

in Friar Tuck's Bar

at Club Fabulous

at Club Desire   on Law and Desire

in Pal's Bar, Bayou St. John   her 28-year-old throat slashed

by a man on his way out the door   [that was Nia]

at the Crescent City Connection

at Show Stopper Tattoos   in back of Spice One

outside the Chat Room

in an overgrown lot   in the neighborhood of Desire

partially charred   [that was Jody]

on Piety

between two vacant houses   the light there has an aura

the smell of sweet olive   so strong

near the corner of Amelia

St. Roch again, a double   before lunchtime

on the sidewalk, faceup   he beheld

a confusion of color

in front of a gutted house   Lower Ninth

Porche was her name

near the tracks

in a FEMA trailer   the9thwardwordman

thence   his mama entered a conglomerate of hurt

vii.

while walking   down Frenchmen about 9:15

on the sidewalk on Lotus near Myrtle

in a grassy area in the Iberville complex

on Frenchmen, again   Dominique, 16

in the middle of the street   near the Black Pearl

Treme   Marquise, 20, Sylvester, 17

on Laharpe   a triple

lying on the street staring at the asphalt moon

under an abandoned house, a French citizen

in Lake Pontchartrain   newlyweds

another on Pleasure Street   in a burning car

on Sunday on Cadillac

on the steps of her Irish Channel home

in a blue Olds on S. Roman, on a porch, N. Roman

eating a raw potato

faceup   looking at the marbled clouds

the 16th this year, on St. Claude   [we're hardly done with June]

when he fell, when she saw him fall   his mama vomited

viii.

in March   two families

on Clouet [Angel; her children, Jamaria, 7

                              Joseph, 4; her sister Malekia, 17]

in Treme,   two Muses:

Jennifer, her sister Monica;   her mother Wanda

under the steps of the porch   of a lime-colored shotgun

ix.

a triple   on Laharpe

three men dressed in black

on the sidewalk, 2500 block of Upperline

among a cluster of trailers

on the sidewalk in the Seventh Ward   from that angle of repose

he could make out the cages

of his mother's Creole tomatoes

crashed   into a handicapped-access ramp

a witness who testified against Bonds

stuffed inside a Metro can   in the Bywater

the Wild Man of the FiYiYi Mardi Gras Indians   his girlfriend

a short-order cook   in a parked car

near the Crescent City Connection

rammed and shot on S. Claiborne   a suspect in another shooting

on N. Tonti   a double

one down on Pleasure St., again

two in one day   on Lizardi

three on Josephine

in Hollygrove, again   a drum major

his countenance drained of dread   and his characteristic optimism

gone flat   [no one dying to live on Josephine]

x.

breathtaken

in the Faubourg Marigny   beaten, burned

dumped in the woods on Dwyer Rd.   he was going into the city

to take care of some business   he told his mama

he would be back   later

yesterday a boy, 17   in the Fair Grounds

this morning, faceup   bleeding out by a light pole

at Terpsichore   [in view of customers

from a convenience store   a clump of uniformed students

a man sitting on his stoop tells   the cub reporter

There's just too much going on around here.]

You are listening to The Problem Child.

It's hot and humid. Overcast again.

Petition to the Bearers of Precious Images
to recollect a few things about him/her

How long ago did you lose your loved one   to this violence
Where was your loved one taken
What time of year, what hour
What was your loved one's relation to you
What was your loved one's given name

Did you have a pet name for your loved one
If you knew your loved one as a child   could you
Pass on a precious image   to a mere bystander to bear
What was your loved one's best physical feature
Could you draw that feature blind
Did your loved one have a sweet tooth
What was your loved one's prized possession
Did you keep a piece of your loved one's clothing
Was your loved one a day person or a night person
Was your loved one a good mimic
Was your loved one a good loser
Did your loved one like beets or rhubarb   or okra or gizzards
Hog jowls [with or without greens]
Did your loved one have a name for you other than your given
Did your loved one ever catch an eel   bare-handed
Could your loved one stand on her head
Do you have any pictures made by him
Did your loved one like to read
Could your loved one tell a story
Was that your loved one's burgundy bike
Did your loved one like the movies
Was there something in school that for
Your loved one was extra
Did your loved one know any lyrics
Did your loved one play a mouth harp
Did your loved one own a gun
Was there anything your loved one liked   to collect
After your loved one was taken   is there anything
Anyone told you about them   [that took you by surprise]
Did your loved one have long feet
Did your loved one have pretty ears
Did your loved one like pockets
Did your loved one wear his hair   in a special way
Did your loved one ever do something   just for you

That made you feel extra
Could your loved one swim on his back   dance, drive
A big piece of machinery
Was your loved one a fast runner   a fast talker
Did your loved one like snowballs   Tabasco, po'boys
Did you say your loved one lies   in the Garden of Memories
Or is she with Our Lady Queen of Peace
Could your loved one tell a joke
What was your loved one's best color
If your loved one was a hurter   can you
Pass a night with feelings   other than regret
Can you lift yourself up
If your loved one never hurt a bug
Can you pass a day without rancor   can you
Lift yourself up   again

Obscurity and Empathy

The left hand rests on the paper.

The hand has entered the frame just below the elbow.

The other hand is in its service.

The left moves along a current that is not visible
and on a signal likewise inaudible, goes still.

For the hand to respond the ink must be black.

There is no watermark.

One nail is broken well below the quick.

The others filed short.
Or chewed.

The hand is drawn to objects.

In another's it becomes pliant
and readily absorbs the moisture of the other's.

It retains the memory of the smell of her infant son's hair.

Everything having been written, the hand has to work hard
to get up in the spaces.

There is no tremor, but the skin is thin and somewhat
crepey.

The veins stand out.

The hand has begun to gesture toward its ghosthood.
Though at times it becomes almost frisky.

The desk is side-lit.

The hand has options, but has chosen to stay
inside its own pale, thin walls.

It has begun to show signs of its own shoddy construction.

The hand is there to express shouts and whispers,
ordinary love,

the afterimage of everything.

From the outside what light leaks through the blind
is blue, blue-grey.

There is a dog.

There is a fan.

The fan is on the dog.

Imaginary Suitcase

This belonged to your mother. Now

it is yours though you have no memory

of her and we'll never know if she wrote it

by herself or copied it down from a book.

In this pouch is a lock of her velvet hair.

Anyone on the square would tell you,

she was a beautiful girl. I know this won't

get you far but when you get to where

you're going, Youngblood, that your days

be long, and your nights release a fleet

of dreams, your love be a trumpet vine.

Pocket every penny that drops and swear off

the sauce that ate the head of your father.

ShallCross

We are walking along a curve

Observed by the hawk

Completing the arc

For us but not by us

Responding to the gravity

Of the bend as we climb

Toward a jagged ridge

Pages fluttered by the softest

Wind as wind slips through

The folding door

Of a listing phone booth

Across the drawbridge

A store called Her Hands

A club called His Room

An out-of-date flier for

A free seminar for the heart

Angelica is rampant

Egrets flock the treetops

The day wears itself away

Against the barbed fencing

A barge goes quietly off course

Cars are sparser now

Crows are everywhere

Getting bigger louder closer

In a well-kept farmhouse

A lid slams down

On a pounded piano

As the words sink into me

You are still young enough

To adopt a xolo

Write an opera on glass

Bed a chimera

Bedazzle and be devoured

The moonroof in your head

Slowly sliding open

To the scent of oleander

The bad gushing out of you

Things in plain sight things hidden

It doesn't make any difference

If I could buffer my fall

Not with my body but my breath

Maybe stay awake for

The appearance of a small angel

Clear frozen beautiful

Like someone from Chicago

Living ocular proof

Of an immense force swooping

Swiftly downward to cool

The coils within coils

Having missed the free seminar

By several decades now

Even the namer of clouds is gone

So whatever I thought

Was tender or true

Left my face a network

Of hatchmarks from a mother

Lost in the exclusion zone

Father felled from the feet up

Son whose brown eyes

Are both sharper and softer

Than either of ours

An impossible child

No one could break or resist

Who has begun to beat his own

Diamondback path

To the edge of his fields

To the edge of his life

As the big clouds are rolling in

I try to herd the worst feelings

I ever felt the worst thoughts

The very worst under one

Warped sheet of metal

A nonbeliever dropped to

A pair of knobby knees

Every other thing reminds me

Of you even a tempera

By a seven-year-old

From Down Under titled

The Driver Sits in the Shade

But What About the Horse

It was something you might

Have said to a family waiting

For a taxi to the historic district

Or a gondola to take them

Off the mountain

Even a milk glass

Of field flowers sensed

You entering the room

Before you dropped me off

On a Lower East Side curb

With my rolling bags of grief

And pretty sheer brassieres

It's starting to seem as if everyone

Were already dead

And looking for my glasses

While Vic plunks out Buckets

Of Rain to a smoke-soaked

Roadhouse of rubes

My disappointment sits

Under the Tree of Disappointment

In a dirty skirt in a ruff

Of dirt the color of dirt

If a hand and it could be my hand

Moves over the bark it touches

Where an arrow passed through the trunk

The mind wills it into reverse

That the shaft of the arrow glide

Soundlessly backward

And the hand it could be your hand

Soothes the welt left by its entry

The air turns the blue of a seldom-worn

Dress left in a closet by the woman

Who opened a notebook

To what must have been your hand

It looked like your striking

Script of course it was your hand

That wrote she doesn't get it

I was never there

Of my own volition

I would have never asked

The grass is strong unlike her

The water unperturbedly furled

The Ladder Tree leans toward me

And then swings out of reach

The ache that will last the rest

Of our lives stiffens into those words

The Tree of Knowledge

Tries to draw off the poison

Without destroying itself

Now who will make the record of us

Who will be the author

Of our blind and bilious hours

Of the silken ear of our years

Who will distinguish our dandruff

From the rest among the gusts of history

Who will turn our maudlin concerns

Into moments of incandescence

Who remember when I was a dirty blond

That hung like a mare's mane

A blond with an even dirtier mouth

And a pent-up anatomy

Your shoe trailing on the ground

Moving gracefully round me

Trying to stir up the hardpan

So thirsty and hot

Who fill us with the tingle

Of animation and of wonder

Who be there glistening

With sweat and forgiveness

Once the stall has been mucked

And re-mucked

The Tree That Owns Itself appears

Sickly but still blossoms

In Vic's hometown along with

The eight feet of earth round it

Which is not enough

Sedated to hopefully endure

The dozers and cranes

When the word turbine wanes

I can hear a bee entering a quince

A shoot of bamboo piercing

The skin of the earth

A black ant climbing a stem

The sound of raw umber

Distinct from burnt

The sound of still water

The sound of a towel

Drifting to the ground

The sound of you rubbing

Oil on someone else's limbs

It is so patently stupid to stick

By a one-stoplight-town dream

To love and be loved to the end

Without ruth or recrimination

Como una estúpida película

We saw at an outdoor theater

In Guerrero standing up

From previews to credits

In a warm downpour

Then I see the quivery

Shadow of my stricken self

Left on a traffic island

At the noisiest intersection

In Buenos Aires

Drowning in the decibels

I don't want you to count

The conks on my trunk

Under the Tree of Conjugal Love

How this feels to be diminished

By one the one mistaken

For the one who would usher

Us away from the Tree

Of Failure and Shame

Beyond the Tree of Deceit

Unfulfillment and Illusion

Into the limbic woods

Of subtle adults-only stuff

Long-playing side-lit up-flickering

Beyond the Tree of Childish Wishes

Past the Tree of Ten Thousand Mistakes

I'm sure there is a word

In English there is always a word

What is that low-flying short-winged bird

Your mother would know

Even if she can't call up its name

They fly alone notwithstanding

They are abundant

But they fly only the breadth of a field

Traveling silently

It is early yet you said I'm going back to my study

A hand reaching toward your half-turned head

Pale sun filtering through the cloud floor

Passing over a tangle of tensions and angularities

A silver band suddenly visible in the grass

The perennials by the shed identifying

Themselves by vibration alone

The light discolored as candelabrum

From a preceding life your Junoesque

Hand turning the handle to a door carved

From a Tree of Tomorrows

Don't shut it I said We lack for nothing

Indissolubly connected

Across the lines of our lives

The once the now the then and again

Casting Deep Shade: An Amble Inscribed to Beech Trees & Co.

COPPER CANYON PRESS, 2019

Poses no significant litter problem.

Ranks as "not particularly outstanding" according to the Forest Service.

Stone Age men dined on beechnuts with their clubby hirsute hands.

Iron Age man made beechnut flour.

Native Americans made beechnut flour.

Most runes were carved in yew but beech was an acceptable substitute.

A recipe for beechnut butter is easy to obtain.

A lot of nutrients in the fruit of chestnut, oak, beech. Same mealy, meaty family.

Can hold a nail but tends to split when nailed.

Can hold a curve.

As in, the turned parts of the "democratic" Windsor chair.

Except when green.

Nut is rich in oil, of pleasant flavor.

The Druids grew wise eating their nuts.

The pollen record keeps going back and back.

Pollen from pre-Roman peats has been found in the UK.

In a dream it signifies wisdom, else, death.

Is brittle.

In aromatherapy, a confidence booster.

Windfirm if the soil is not shallow.

Limbs low.

Beech, *Fagus*. Family Fagaceae. Alternating leaves of the *sylvatica* (European) crenated, of the *grandifolia* (American) crenulated; the former a little wavy, the latter a little toothy. Deciduous, monoecious, smooth, silver-grey bark, fruits three-angle nuts, in a bristly involucre, averaging 80 feet, can live 500 years, though standard is 200–300.

American beech (*Fagus grandifolia*) is not the priority here, only because it is rarely among the beeches I see daily where I live in southern New England. Their masses having been greatly diminished since settlers grasped that they grew in soil good for farming.

At the upper end of the Appalachian Trail in the Adirondacks, long after the settlers cleared the land and killed off enough timber wolf and cougar, deer populations began to snowball. Logging took much birch and maple, beech becoming dominant. By the 1960s, beech bark disease (BBD) took out 9 of 10 trees in massive chunks of forest, with the new shoots carrying the same doomed DNA.

The disease has moved into lower elevations. A student at the University of Tennessee studied clonality in the beech gaps in 2006. She found zero resistance to BBD. *Zero.*

In the early nineties, the Adirondacks were beech-death country.

Where beech bark disease has struck, smaller, weaker, or soon-to-be-infected offspring follow.

Ghost trees are those dying of beech bark. They turn white.
(I personally have never seen a ghost.)

Along the southern Appalachian forest trail there are more tree species than any other forest in North America.

In the Pleistocene, beech spanned the continent.

Stands and groves and mixed woods are still not so rare.

The European or common beech (*Fagus sylvatica*) is, however, at hand, here specifically being Rhode Island, though it has never, as the keeper of the Arnold Arboretum in Boston, MA, told me, been known to go rogue.

Would that it would.

Escapes, it is written, are to be expected.

*

The dawn redwoods on our block in Rhode Island tower over a neighbor's 20-year-old neocolonial house and the immaculate, uneventful lawn the twins occupy. I am both glad and sad that they are here. They make the house look fictitious. They demand so much more water than I imagine they can draw here. Classified as critically endangered. Yet they appear healthy. A volunteer can be glimpsed in the back corner of their lot. Ready to step in when the elders cross over.

There is a small stand of *Fagus grandifolia* in Arnold Arboretum in Boston, and I visited a cluster in Lost Valley in the Arkansas Ozarks when I was there in May for some literary confab. I mentioned beeches to a woman in Little Rock and the next morning she came back with an email of detailed directions from one whom I would call an extreme nurseryman from the Arkansas Delta, repatriated in Carroll County (where my father was born; which we were encouraged to call the Holy Land).

*

In Memphis there are estate-sized magnolias. In New York City, the squirrels and the trees both look pretty beat, though Central Park in the rain can still feel restorative. In San Francisco, there are the towering eucalyptuses and profuse rhododendrons in Golden Gate Park, palms on Dolores and at the Artaud theater, New Zealand bottlebrushes, and streetside strawberry trees. In Dolores Hidalgo, state of Guanajuato, the flamboyanes and jacarandas and mesquites and my first pomegranate in the courtyard of the Museo Casa de Hidalgo. (While Miguel Hidalgo's bell-tolling alarm and great grita de Dolores are credited with inaugurating their revolution, he was in much deeper than that. The good padre was a full-fledged motivator of the revolt, for which his head was displayed on a spike in Guanajuato.)

It is also written of Dolores Hidalgo that a tree grown from sapling from the Árbol de la Noche Triste, a Montezuma cypress (*Ahuehuete*), stands in the main plaza. It celebrates Cortés's defeat in the Aztec revolt in 1520. However, Montezuma died in the fight, and Cortés escaped by the hair of his chinny chin chin. When living in Dolores Hidalgo, I enjoyed the company of an outstanding tree in the plaza and the ruction of oversized birds that weighted down its limbs in the evening while my beloved and I chomped on charcoaled corn rubbed with red pepper and lime juice.

Then there is the Montezuma cypress, El Árbol del Tule, in Santa María del Tule, Oaxaca. Words don't come close. Never have. Never will.

Were I a diviner of children's books, I would compose a multigenerational Gongorismo chronicle from the point of view of the creatures who have burrowed, nested, and sported in the shelter of that spectacular tree, somewhere between 1,400 and 3,000 years old (opinions differ). I would have to consume many a magic mushroom to touch the wonder.

Second Monday of October El Árbol is given a party.

El Árbol del Tule enjoys the title of the world's fattest.

In the USA, we the people enjoy the title of the world's fattest.

Water
　　　　is an issue
Pollution
　　　　is an issue
The table
　　　　is dropping
The cars
　　　　they are
breeding

Sometimes nothing to do but gawk. Openmouthed. Bug-eyed. Gobsmacked.

*

Home in Illinois, Lincoln liked to read under a beech. Lincoln liked to read period. For all we know he may have liked to look at dirty flip-books under the ample canopy of a solitary beech.

Though Lincoln was known to have enjoyed reading under a beech, it is apparently not true that he and his son Tad played and read under a copper beech at the cottage on the grounds of the Soldiers' Home. This is where Lincoln drafted the Emancipation Proclamation, and the kids could play mumble-the-whatever-the-hell-it-is-peg. This is where he rode Old Bob, grey shawl over his own grey shoulders, and though usually accompanied by a cavalry detail, did once have his high hat shot through. The tree, real enough, was probably not big enough at the time to provide shade for the idle, bookish type.

A copper beech is planted in front of his seated statue in Louisville, where with bronze book balanced on his knee, pried open by a bronze finger, he watches the Ohio roll on, where he first saw slaves unloaded, and was put wise to his revulsion toward the peculiar institution.

They are very beautiful, firm, and perfect leaves, unspotted and not eaten by insects, of a handsome, clear leather-color, like a book bound in calf. Crisp and elastic.   Thoreau

There is a Corot of a woman lying down reading in a beech grove. Really the painting is of the trees. She just happens to be in the lower-left corner, barefoot, loose-tressed, corseted. From here, the pages that absorb the woman are just gobbledygook.

Greek proverb: A civilization flourishes when people plant trees under which they will never sit—there may be more than one possible translation of that one.

African proverb: Roots do not know what a leaf has in mind.

Everytime the tree works the leaves dream.   Frank Stanford

That mono-focal experience of the *bok* is the heart and soul of what it means to read.

*

To others I say I am visiting these individuals (which doesn't mean I carry on a delusional dialogue with them like poor Richard Nixon wandering the White House halls talking to the portraits). It means I go to pay my respects, and discreetly to ogle. My approach is close to ceremonial—split-open ribcage, palpitating heart in hand.

~

True, I sappily envisioned an evening with old friends under hovering lanterns, among these sensational sessile beings, branches limbing low, flirty laughter, prosecco, whitefish and silver queen corn, blackberries, and enough caffeine and dark chocolate to steer one and all home without incident. I waken repeatedly to gnarly misgivings and adversarial imaginings—with developers, apparatchiks, celebrities, lobbyists, an endless cavalcade of the Nouveau Gilded Agers—in flaming dread of *us,* the next annihilating asteroid.

On a recent flight returning to California from DC, I asked the young man seated next to me, a Malek's Tree Service patch on his khaki shirt pocket, studying a book with a man on the cover straddling the branches of a eucalyptus, What made you decide to get into tree work. Let's see, he said, I thought to myself, I like nature, I like to climb things, and I love power tools.

water   *minerals*   *air*   *light*

Why Leave You So Soon Gone

Ah well   Be well   Be iron   On rock

sharpen yourself   Remember   heat goes out the top

Follow thought   migration of stars   Detach

from the surrounding sound   Be resistant

to disease and evil   Take the path worn by the walker

the dreamline   Take the dreamline   inalienable map

of rivers and lovers   in subtle and effortless tones   Say yes

when the month begins   Take ginger   Chew garlic

If you won't wear the watch cap   We miss   Remember

your hood   Don't forget the subjunctive   the usual nostrums

Never a glove   So like your father   Listen to me

You're going to need this   way up there   Don't forget

The tip jar   You're going to need   When you're moving

at the speed of loneliness   and your papers pile up in drifts

Call back later   your words   breaking up in this ear

Tell the truth   the trees tell   as their boughs bend

to the forces   leaves spray in all directions   their limbs rend

as they come crashing   across invisible fencing

the privet   the shingles   the insulated glass   the horsehair

plaster crumbles in my head   their leaves shattering the light

Sharpen yourself   on rock   Say yes   Don't forget

Index of Titles

Abandon Yourself to That Which Is Inevitable, 10

Against the Encroaching Greys, 6

Alla Breve Loving, 30

Amarillo Poem, 206

Amnesiac, 33

Approximately Forever, 83

"Because conditions are ideal for crowing," 78

Because Fulfillment Awaits, 84

Breathtaken, 210

A Brief and Blameless Outline of the Ontogeny of Crow, 77

Clockmaker with Bad Eyes, 47

from Collaborating, 119

from Concerning Complexity, 117

Crescent, 91

Detail from *What No One Could Have Told Them*, 71

End Sheet, 201

End Thoughts, 156

Everything Good Between Men and Women, 92

Falling Beasts, 44

from Five of Us Drove to Horatio:, 121

Flame, 94

Foretold, 43

Further Adventures with You, 58

her disquietude absorbed., 17

Imaginary Suitcase, 229

In a Piercing and Sucking Species, 90

In a Word, a World [Although I take a special pleasure], 187

In a Word, a World [I also admit a weakness], 189

In a Word, a World [I know the adjective], 186

In a Word, a World [I like nouns], 192

In a Word, a World [I love the nouns], 191

In a Word, a World [I love them all], 183

In a Word, a World [The mother word], 193

in our only time., 124

from Just Looking:, 118

Key Episodes from an Earthly Life, 88

Libretto, 46

Light Bulb Poem, 205

Like Some Dislocation of Reality, 8

Like the Circles Under Your Eyes, 15

Living, 72

Margaret Kaelin Vittitow, 29

Morning Star, 93

My American Scrawl [Increasingly indecisive], 184

My American Scrawl [Poetry requires movement], 190

The night before the sentence is carried out, 38

The not knowing whether what you've set down is any good, 188

Obedience of the Corpse, 37

Oblique Gaze, 19

Obscurity and Empathy, 227

On the Eve of Their Mutually Assured Destruction:, 79

One night last summer, 12

Oneness, 85

from Op-Ed, 115

Our Dust, 65

Poem Before Breakfast, 28

Poem from the End of Old Wire Road, 209

Poem with a Dead Tree, 208

Poem with Some Water Damage, 207

"Poems are my building projects," 185

Poetry and Parenting, 122

Posing Without Glasses, 27

Questionnaire in January, 194

Rains, 20

Re: Happiness, in pursuit thereof, 145

Remarks on Color, 63

from Rising, Falling, Hovering, 146

The Same Water Everywhere, 13

Scratch Music, 53

Sculptor and Model, 21

Selected translations of an abecedarian, 23

ShallCross, 230

Stripe for Stripe, 127

This Couple, 55

This Much I Know:, 123

Tours, 39

Two Hearts in a Forest, 56

Unconditional Love Song, 9

Voice of the Ridge, 80

Voices That Never Arrive, 22

Wages of Love, 51

What Keeps, 87

What No One Could Have Told Them, 68

Why Don't You Go Sit Under a Big Tree, 5

Why Leave You So Soon Gone, 257

Acknowledgments

Grateful acknowledgment to the editors of the following publications that have published selections of C.D. Wright's uncollected work: *Conjunctions, Harper's Magazine, The New Yorker.*

The editors would also like to thank Deborah Luster, Denny Moers, Michael Ondaatje and Linda Spalding, Susie Schlesinger, and Brecht Wright Gander, as well as Joseph Bednarik, David Caligiuri, Marie Landau, Alison Lockhart, Jessica Roeder, and Rowan Sharp.

About the Author

C.D. Wright grew up in Arkansas. She was the author of more than a dozen collections of poetry and prose and a recipient of numerous awards, including a MacArthur Fellowship. *One With Others [a little book of her days]* won the National Book Critics Circle Award and the Lenore Marshall Prize and was a finalist for the National Book Award. Her book *Rising, Falling, Hovering* won the 2009 International Griffin Poetry Prize. Wright was married to writer/ translator Forrest Gander and taught at Brown University. She unexpectedly passed away in her sleep on January 12, 2016.

About the Editors

Forrest Gander lived with C.D. Wright for thirty-five years, beginning in 1981. Their child, now a man, is the artist Brecht Wright Gander. Forrest, born in the Mojave Desert, is a translator/writer with degrees in geology and literature. He has received the Pulitzer Prize, the Best Translated Book Award, and fellowships from the Library of Congress, the Guggenheim Foundation, and United States Artists.

Michael Wiegers edited *The Essential W.S. Merwin* and *What About This: Collected Poems of Frank Stanford,* as well as *A House Called Tomorrow: Fifty Years of Poetry from Copper Canyon Press.* He has worked as C.D. Wright's editor for thirty years and is currently writing a book about the poet W.S. Merwin.

Special Thanks

Copper Canyon Press is deeply grateful to the following individuals whose generous vision and love of poetry made *The Essential C.D. Wright* possible:

Anonymous
Zeinab Masud Agha
S. Craig Alexander
Kazim Ali
Giana Angelillo
Victoria Barcott
Twanna P. Bolling
David Brewster and Mary Kay
    Sneeringer
Michelle Castleberry
Justin Chimka
Jane Stephens Rosenthal Cooke
Cheney Crow
Michael Detto
Jane Ellis and Jack Litewka
Grace Ferguson
Jim and Susan Finnegan
Forrest Gander
Christine Gedye
Dan Gerber
Mimi Gonzalez/noemi rose
Maurine Haltiner
Brenda Hillman
Holly J. Hughes and John Pierce
Janet Isserlis
Edward J.
Julie Christine Johnson
Alice Jones
Jack Saebyok Jung

George Kalamaras
Ken Kaufman
Ben Lerner
Todd Parker Lowe
Deborah Luster
Jami Macarty
Michelle Mankins
Stephanie Mankins
Sati Mookherjee
Joseph P. Morra
karla k. morton
Daniel Nasman
Allen Nishikawa
Jill Pearlman
Lee Perron
James Pickrel
Jennifer M. Pierson
John and Kathy Popko
Valerie Popp and Michael Lin
Michael Quattrone
Brendan Quinn
Shann Ray
Jessica Reed
Alan C. Reese
Victoria Reynolds
Martha Ronk
Sarah Ruhl
Javier Sandoval
Kristyn J. Saunders

Timothy Schaffner

Rick Simonson

Michael Smallwood

Chrissy Stegman

Jennifer Sperry Steinorth

Ed and Katherine Wich Sugden

Arthur Sze

Chase Twichell

Dan Waggoner

Linda Walsh and Keith Cowan

Emily Warn

Caroline Noble Whitbeck

Patrick Whitgrove and Mona Baroudi

Nathan Wirth

Marion C. Zinkievich

Poets for Poetry

Copper Canyon Press poets are at the center of all our efforts as a nonprofit publisher. Poets not only create the art that defines our books, but they read and teach the books we publish. Many are also generous donors who believe in financially supporting the larger poetry community of Copper Canyon Press. For decades, our poets have quietly donated their royalties, have directly engaged in our fundraising campaigns, and have made personal donations in support of the next generation. Their support has encouraged the innovative risk-taking that sustains and furthers the art form.

The donor-poets who have contributed to the Press since 2023 include:

Jonathan Aaron	Jennifer L. Knox
Kelli Russell Agodon	Ted Kooser
Pamela Alexander	Deborah Landau
Joyce Harrington Bahle	Sung-Il Lee
Ellen Bass	Ben Lerner
Mark Bibbins	Dana Levin
Sherwin Bitsui	Heather McHugh
Marianne Boruch	Jane Miller
Laure-Anne Bosselaar	Lisa Olstein
Cyrus Cassells	Gregory Orr
Peter Cole and Adina Hoffman	Eric Pankey
Elizabeth J. Coleman	Kevin Prufer
John Freeman	Paisley Rekdal
Forrest Gander	James Richardson
Jenny George	Alberto Ríos
Daniel Gerber	David Romtvedt
Julian Gewirtz	Natalie Shapero
Jorie Graham	Arthur Sze
Robert and Carolyn Hedin	Elaine Terranova
Bob Hicok	Chase Twichell
Ha Jin	Ocean Vuong
Jaan Kaplinski	Connie Wanek-Dentinger
Laura Kasischke	Emily Warn

Poetry is vital to language and living. Since 1972, Copper Canyon Press has published extraordinary poetry from around the world to engage the imaginations and intellects of readers, writers, booksellers, librarians, teachers, students, and donors.

WE ARE GRATEFUL FOR THE MAJOR SUPPORT PROVIDED BY:

TO LEARN MORE ABOUT UNDERWRITING
COPPER CANYON PRESS TITLES,
PLEASE CALL 360-385-4925 EXT. 105

WE ARE GRATEFUL FOR THE MAJOR SUPPORT PROVIDED BY:

Anonymous

Jill Baker and Jeffrey Bishop

Anne and Geoffrey Barker

Donna Bellew

Lisha Bian

Will Blythe

John Branch

Diana Broze

John R. Cahill

Sarah J. Cavanaugh

Keith Cowan and Linda Walsh

Peter Currie

Geralyn White Dreyfous

The Evans Family

Mimi Gardner Gates

Gull Industries Inc.
    on behalf of William True

Carolyn and Robert Hedin

David and Jane Hibbard

Bruce S. Kahn

Phil Kovacevich and Eric Wechsler

Maureen Lee and Mark Busto

Ellie Mathews and Carl Youngmann
    as The North Press

Larry Mawby and Lois Bahle

Petunia Charitable Fund and
    adviser Elizabeth Hebert

Suzanne Rapp and Mark Hamilton

Adam and Lynn Rauch

Emily and Dan Raymond

Joseph C. Roberts

Cynthia Sears

Kim and Jeff Seely

Tree Swenson

Julia Sze

Barbara and Charles Wright

In honor of C.D. Wright
    from Forrest Gander

Caleb Young as C. Young Creative

The dedicated interns and faithful
    volunteers of Copper Canyon Press

The pressmark for Copper Canyon Press
suggests entrance, connection, and interaction
while holding at its center
an attentive, dynamic space for poetry.

This book is set in Adobe Garamond Pro.
Book design by Phil Kovacevich.
Printed on archival-quality paper.